D0445323

A GUIDE TO THE COLLECTING
AND CARE OF ORIGINAL PRINTS

BOOKS BY CARL ZIGROSSER

A
GUIDE
TO THE
COLLECTING
AND CARE
OF
ORIGINAL
PRINTS

by
CARL ZIGROSSER
and
CHRISTA M. GAEHDE

SPONSORED BY
The Print Council of America

CROWN PUBLISHERS, INC., NEW YORK

Contents

v

A GUIDE TO THE COLLECTING
AND CARE OF ORIGINAL PRINTS

.

Preface

THE KERNEL of the present work is contained in the booklet
What Is an Original Print? published by the Print Council
in 1961. The original pamphlet, edited by Joshua Binion
Cahn, was a statement of the principles underlying the thorny
problem of original versus reproduction—original prints by
artists versus the spurious productions that masquerade under
their name. The widespread response to the booklet has in-
dicated to the Council that there is real need for a work of
larger scope, not only to consider the question of the original
print but also to provide an introduction to print collecting
in general.

As a consequence, the largest part of this work is addressed
to the collector and his needs. An introduction to prints and
collecting is followed by a short bibliography, a glossary
of terms and techniques, and by a paper on the care and
conservation of prints, written by the restorer-expert Christa
M. Gaehde. The case of the contemporary original print is
treated in two chapters, one on the current problem and the
other on the historical background.

The chapter "The Artist and the Print Market" closes with a declaration on original works of graphic art by the International Association of Plastic Arts, UNESCO House, Paris, issued at its Third International Congress, in Vienna, 1960. In the drafting of this resolution the Print Council played a part through correspondence between Berto Lardera, Secretary-General of the Association, and Theodore J. H. Gusten, Executive Secretary of the Print Council of America, and through participation at the Congress by Gabor Peterdi, special representative of the Council. The formulation of the Council's Guide for Artists' Procedures has been assisted by the advice and comment of numerous practicing artists, including Antonio Frasconi, Jerome Kaplan, Misch Kohn, Mauricio Lasansky, Gabor Peterdi, Rudy Pozzatti, and Benton Spruance.

The chapter "The Dealer and the Print Market" has been augmented by the specification of a Code of Dealers' Standards. An advisory committee of print dealers assisted in the drafting of the declaration. The chapter also discusses auctions and appraisals from the dealers' point of view.

Many of my colleagues on the Print Council have helped me by their constructive criticism in the writing of the booklet. The participation of Egbert Haverkamp-Begemann, Alan Fern, Jacob Kainen, and Lessing J. Rosenwald has been so close as to make them almost collaborators. Kneeland McNulty, Sinclair Hitchings, Ebria Feinblatt, Joshua Cahn, and Theodore Gusten have given valuable advice. In the compilation of technical terms I have been aided by the publications of A. M. Hind, J. A. Bender, Una Johnson, Will Barnet, and Harry Sternberg, as well as by those enumerated in the text. For all their generous assistance, I am most grateful, since they have helped to make this a better and more authoritative book. The mistakes, alas, will still be my own.

CARL ZIGROSSER

[2]

I

For the Collector

WHAT ARE FINE PRINTS?

THERE HAVE been collectors of prints for hundreds of years. What are prints, and why are they collected? The word *print* has only five letters, but it stands for a great many things. Literally, it means anything that is printed; and our life is surrounded by a multitude of printed things—for instance, postage stamps, paper money, stock certificates, illustrations in books, newspapers and magazines, photographs, posters and advertisements, color reproductions of famous paintings, and the like. But we do not collect all these things, although stamps, money, and stock certificates have been collected with profit on occasion.

There are, however, certain kinds of prints that are collected because they are works of art. One might call them "printed pictures," and the name is both descriptive and significant. The artist in general has many mediums in which to work: he may create oil paintings, watercolors, drawings, sculptures in wood, stone, or bronze—or he may make printed pictures. The medium he chooses depends upon his inclination and training, but also upon the audience he intends to address. If he contemplates a single purchaser for his handiwork, he will draw, paint in oil or watercolor, or carve in wood or stone, because each work in these categories is unique, and can be possessed by only one purchaser. If he projects a wider circle of future owners—involving not one but numerous originals, each of which is truly an original—he will model and cast statues in bronze, or he will make fine prints, such as etchings, engravings, woodcuts, or lithographs. The essential characteristic of a fine print is that it is a printed picture. The key to the method of making a print lies in the creation of a master design on a suitable medium, such as, for example, a wood block or copperplate, which can be inked and printed to produce a quantity of identical prints. It is a device to produce multi-originals. The unique thing about prints is that they are not unique. In a sense, printmaking is a democratic form of art, for it enables not one but many persons to own and enjoy the same work of art. If an artist were to receive $1,000 for either a unique picture, such as an oil painting, or for his work that could be produced in an edition of, let us say, ten, the purchaser would pay $1,000 for the oil painting but $100 for the printed picture. One cannot buy a very distinguished oil painting for $100, but one can purchase an excellent original print in color or black and white for that amount, not only by contemporary artists but even by many famous old masters.

It is not the medium but the aesthetic intention that creates a work of art and gives it value. One can paint the side of a barn or one can paint a picture; the medium is the same, namely, oil colors. Similarly, one can cast a cooking utensil or cast a beautiful statue. Every medium has both utilitarian and aesthetic functions. This is especially true of printmaking.

In its early development, printmaking was quantitatively more utilitarian than artistic, furnishing (quite apart from religious imagery and other pictorial subject matter) all the illustrations in printed books of science, technology, botany, architecture, models for furniture, textiles and costumes—that vast storehouse of visual knowledge about *things* upon which our civilization and culture are based. But throughout the history of graphic art, there have always been some artists who have made original prints more for pleasure and delectation than for utility. These are more or less the works we collect today.

It may be said, therefore, that prints in general—what William M. Ivins called the precisely duplicable image—have played a major role in the shaping of our culture. Prints over the ages have been appreciated or found useful for many different reasons, some of which are not necessarily aesthetic. But fine or original prints, made by artists themselves, have all the characteristics and virtues of original works of art; and, owing to the nature of the graphic processes, are multioriginals; that is to say, they exist in more than one example, each of which is an original.

THE TECHNIQUES OF PRINTMAKING

Several principles or methods of duplication have been devised to produce prints in quantity. The first and oldest is the relief method, so called because the design stands out in relief. The design is drawn upon a flat piece of wood, and every area except the design itself is cut away with a knife or other tool to a depth down to about an eighth of an inch. The projecting design is inked and a sheet of paper laid on it. By rubbing, or by vertical pressure on the back of the paper, the design is transferred to the paper to produce a woodcut or wood engraving.

The second process is called intaglio. In principle it is the reverse of the relief method. The design is incised below the plane surface of a metal plate by means of an engraving tool or acid. A stiff ink is forced into the furrowed lines, and the rest of the plate is wiped clean. A dampened sheet of paper is laid over the plate, and the two are run through a roller press under high pressure. The resulting print is called an engraving or an etching. These are the so-called intaglio linear processes. There are also the intaglio tone processes, mezzotint, stipple, and aquatint, to produce more or less uniform tonal areas by means of minute dots instead of lines. They are described in greater detail in the glossary of technical terms in Chapter IV.

The third method is known as planographic or surface printing. It makes use of the antipathy of water and grease to create a design on a certain kind of smooth stone slab, for example. If, for instance, a line is drawn with a greasy crayon on the stone and the stone dampened with water, the greasy mark will repel the water, but the untouched areas of stone will absorb the water. After an operation to prevent the greasy mark from spreading, a greasy ink may be rolled on the stone. The greasy ink will be repelled by the dampened areas but will stick to the greasy parts. The inked design can be transferred to a sheet of paper by running the paper and the slab through a special kind of press to produce a lithograph.

The fourth duplicating principle can be described as a hole in a masking surface, in other words, a stencil. If any shape is cut in a masking material, such as a very thin sheet of copper or celluloid, and if that sheet is laid on a piece of paper, and pigment brushed over it, then an exact replica of the hole will appear in pigment on the paper beneath. Though the process has been used for coloring prints in quantity for many centuries, it was adapted for artists' use about twenty-five years ago. The improvement consists in creating the equivalent of a stencil on a piece of silk or other textile stretched on a wooden frame. Silk-screen printing, as it has been called, has been much used for commercial or reproductive purposes. The name *serigraph* has been reserved for original prints made by artists. The process does not involve the use of a press, but the meaning of the phrase *to print* has long since been enlarged to include numerous operations not dependent upon the pressure of a press, such as, for instance, the printing of photographs or the printing of a wood block by hand with a spoon.

The above summary of the four major methods of making printed pictures is limited to a consideration of general principles of duplication. All the techniques of printmaking are described in greater detail in the Glossary in Chapter IV.

THE ADVANTAGES OF COLLECTING PRINTS

One great advantage possessed by fine prints has already been mentioned, namely, that their relatively low cost enables many people of moderate means to own and cherish genuine works of art. Indeed, prints and perhaps drawings are about the only bona fide works by the old masters that most people can ever hope to obtain, since the great and unique masterpieces of the past are exclusively within the province of museums or very rich collectors. Prints also enable many to share the adventure of collecting the art of their time. There are, however, still other advantages. One is that their relatively small scale is peculiarly adapted to human size and habitation. They have an intimate appeal not possessed by large oil paintings. They are ideally suited for wall decoration in the home. On the wall, they do not demand the heavy frames or special lighting arrangements often required by dark oils. Since prints can be stored in Solander boxes (see

Chapter VII) when unframed, they do not present any serious storage problem when not on display. The beginning art collector is well advised to start by collecting prints, because he can live with and try out various kinds and styles of art without making too great an investment, and thus eventually discover in which direction his taste and inclinations lie. In the beginning it is not advisable to buy at auction. At an auction, the amateur is usually competing with experts. He can have little recourse if a mistake has been made. The "bargains" that a dealer passes up are few and far between.

ADVICE TO COLLECTORS

How should a beginner proceed to collect? It is a question often asked. The voice of experience would probably answer as follows: It is best to adopt an experimental attitude. Start with something that appeals to you for any reason whatever, as, for instance, because you have read about it or seen it at a friend's house. Look at it, study it, learn what you can about it and the artist who made it. Then go on to buy others in the same way. Have the courage of your own taste. You will make mistakes—everyone does at first—but mistakes are expendable. Only by daring to make mistakes will you learn from your collecting. You will find that some prints, like old friends, wear well, whereas in others the emotive potential is soon exhausted. The latter will become the mistakes for you, and can be eliminated.

When confronted with something new, do not make a snap judgment; give it the benefit of the doubt. Try to find out what the artist intended. Remember, it may have taken an artist twenty years to arrive at a mode of expression: you cannot dispose of it in twenty seconds. On the other hand, you are not compelled to like it just because it is new or because some critic told you to. There are so many works of

[8]

art in the world that you could not possibly respond to them all. No one could. It is fortunate that we do not all like the same thing! You are having a personal experience; you are cultivating your own taste; you are building up your own collection for pleasure and enlightenment. Some people combine business with pleasure. Do not—the plea is urgent—do not collect prints with an eye to profit. If you must combine the two, it would be better to collect that form of print known as the stock certificate. Rather, let your investment be in pure and disinterested enjoyment.

Art is literally priceless—that is to say, without price or beyond price. Art cannot be measured by money. Contemporary art is equated with money only because the artist has to live. It sometimes happens that prints appreciate in monetary value. If you own such prints, accept the fact gladly as unanticipated increment, but do not base your strategy of collecting upon that factor. Buy prints because you love them and not because you calculate they will earn money for you. Let your dividends be solely in terms of the imagination and spirit.

Bibliography

A short list of introductory works available in English on the history, techniques, and appreciation of prints. The titles are arranged alphabetically by authors. Monographs on individual artists are not included.

Auvil, Kenneth. *Serigraphy: Silk Screen Techniques for the Artist*, 1965, paperback.

Brunner, Felix. *Handbook of Graphic Reproduction Processes*, 1962.
> An extensive survey of techniques and their identification.

Curwen, Harold. *Processes of Graphic Reproduction in Printing*, 1958.
> Both fine arts and process techniques.

Getlein, Frank and Dorothy. *The Bite of the Print*, 1964.
> An introduction to prints by way of their social meaning.

Hayter, S. W. *About Prints*, 1962.
> A highly personal comment by a modern master.

Hind, A. M. *Guide to the Processes and Schools of Engraving*, 1952.
> A well-ordered syllabus in a British Museum pamphlet of 52 pages.

——. *An Introduction to a History of Woodcuts*, 1963, 2 volumes, paperback.

———. *A History of Engraving and Etching*, 1963, paperback.
This and the work above are standard histories with extensive bibliographies.

Ivins, William M. *How Prints Look*, 1962, paperback.
Magnified photographs of details of prints with commentary on techniques.

———. *Prints and Books*, 1926.
Essays by a great scholar who carried his learning lightly.

Lumsden, Ernest. *The Art of Etching*, 1962, paperback.
The technique, with a well-written and informative historical survey.

Mayor, A. Hyatt. *Guide to the Print Collections*, Metropolitan Museum of Art, 1964, paperback.
A concise but well-balanced introduction to the history of fine prints.

———. *Prints and People: A Social History of Printed Pictures*, Metropolitan Museum of Art, 1971.
A social history of printed pictures.

Peterdi, Gabor. *Printmaking*, 1959.
Modern techniques for artists, clearly described.

Sachs, Paul J. *Modern Prints and Drawings*, 1954.
An introduction to nineteenth- and twentieth-century graphic art by a well-known collector and teacher.

Stubbe, Wolf. *Graphic Art of the Twentieth Century*, 1962.
A sumptuous review of modern prints, chiefly European.

Weitenkampt, Frank. *How to Appreciate Prints*, 1942.
An old-fashioned but still useful introduction, arranged by techniques.

Zigrosser, Carl. *The Appeal of Prints*, 1970.
An appreciation of artist prints, with comparisons of old and modern styles, illustrated.

———. *Prints, Thirteen Essays on the Art of the Print*, 1962.
By the directors of the Print Council and other scholars, edited by C. Zigrosser.

II

The Print as an Original

ORIGINAL VERSUS REPRODUCTION

THE INVENTION of photography and the subsequent development of the photomechanical reproductive processes (such as photogravure, line and halftone engraving, photolithography, collotype, and the like) have brought the technique of reproduction to a high state of perfection. There is hardly any object that cannot be reproduced in a facsimile of illusionary exactness. The processes have been much used to reproduce famous paintings in museums; and such facsimiles have often been used as home wall decorations. In the home, they seem almost as good as the original. Almost, but not quite! Actually, they have neither the texture nor the color nor the scale of the original oil painting. Their appeal is largely associative: they serve as a reminder of a famous work of art. Of course, they can be better than some other kinds of framed decorations or better than none at all; they can reassure people, who feel that their taste is not developed, that they have chosen something artistic. But there is little intrinsic value in such reproductions, and little nourishment for the imagination always inherent in any real work of art.

The essential difference between a photomechanical reproduction and a fine print lies in the word *original*. One may ask with reference to a color reproduction: Where is the original? and receive the correct answer that the original is a painting by So and So in the collection of such and such a museum. But one cannot give the same answer with reference to an artist's etching. There is no mythical original of which the print in question would be a replica. One cannot consider the copperplate the original, or the preliminary drawing study with its sketchy lines, granted that the artist had made one (often he has not). These are but the preliminary steps in the production of the finished etching, which is the perfect embodiment of the artist's creative intention. The print itself is the original. If a collector wants to have original works of art in his home, he should not buy reproductions.

It is obvious that considerable confusion exists regarding the meaning of the word *original*. When it is used as a noun it refers to an object, as for instance when we say of a print that there are many originals, whereas of a painting or carving there is only one. The usage probably arose as a shortened figure of speech: *original* came to stand for *original work of art*. Thus, there are originals and copies of originals, either manual or photomechanical. When used as an adjective, *original* has a meaning peculiar to the graphic arts. When we speak of an *original* print, we mean that the artist both conceived and executed it. In a *reproductive* print, on the other hand, one printmaker has copied another artist's design. Reproductive prints are therefore a branch of copies in general. Such copies are not necessarily bad: many of the great prints of the past are translations into print form of famous artists' work. Our present age tends to set a high value on originality for its own sake. A further discussion of this complex problem and its beginnings may be found in Chapter III, "The Historical Background of Originality."

As long as reproductions are confined to the works of masters long since dead, there is little possibility of misrepresentation. They are obviously reproductions, whether facsimiles by photomechanical means or copies by competent craftsmen. But in the contemporary field, in view of the prestige attached to original prints and the great demand for them, some doubt might exist whether the picture was made by the artist or by other means. One of the greatest sources of confusion is that photomechanical reproductions are very often loosely labeled as prints. They are prints, to be sure, in that they are printed, but they are not fine or original prints, made by the artist's own hand. If they appear and are sold with the artist's signature in pencil, either forged or genuine, they are nonetheless mechanical mass productions, with no aesthetic value and with little monetary worth, except insofar as an artist's autograph, if genuine, has value.

It is obvious that the practice of signing prints and the whole concept of originality should be clarified. It is not reprehensible for an artist to sign a mechanical reproduction of his work, if he wishes, the justification being that he has inspected the reproduction and approves of its quality. But if there is no indication that it is a reproduction, it might easily be mistaken for a signed proof—that is to say, an original print by him. For the artist's pencil signature has come to mean, in the public mind, a guarantee of authenticity and a sign that the work was executed by the artist. Similarly, it is not unethical for an artist to sign in pencil a copy made by someone else of his work, provided that the print is clearly labeled a copy. If the copyist is not given full credit for his share in the work, it could easily be assumed that the print was by the artist himself.

[15]

FRAUDULENT PRACTICES

Whenever there is a great demand, there is the impulse to supply it either legitimately or illegitimately. This has happened with the demand for original prints. The extraordinary vogue of the School of Paris has led many people to want to own original works by Picasso, Braque, Leger, Miró, Matisse, Chagall, and others, far in excess of what is available. The sharp practices range from ambiguous representations to outright fraud. Some of the types and examples are described below. It should constantly be kept in mind that such spurious prints represent only the smallest fraction of the total legitimate production. If their existence is stressed here, it is because they represent an abuse to be corrected—the one tiny flaw in the whole worthy enterprise.

Certain photomechanical color reproductions, signed and sometimes numbered by the artist, published chiefly in France at relatively high prices, have been represented by dealers, either deliberately or unwittingly through ignorance, as original prints. They have also appeared in many auction sales without precise description.

Similarly, certain reproductive color prints have been made in lithograph or intaglio by an anonymous craftsman who has copied or adapted a finished watercolor or oil painting by a well-known artist. The artist has signed and in many cases numbered the limited edition of the print, but the name of the craftsman does not appear. There may have been various degrees of participation by the artist in the work. In some instances, the artist has actively collaborated in the adaptation of his own *maquette,* or sketch, by working on the plates or stones, and by "proving" and approving the color separations. Such prints can legitimately be called original. But in other instances the artist, either unaware of the implications or complacent in response to the solicitation of an entrepreneur, has left the entire operation in the hands of the expert craftsman. There have been cases where blank sheets of paper, to the number of the edition, have been sent to the artist out of town, and then returned with the artist's pencil signature affixed in a specified space, even before the printing of the picture had commenced. Even the excuse that the artist had signed the print because he approved the quality of the printing would not hold in this extreme instance of misrepresentation.

Certain prints, technically original but printed in large numbers, have also been sold in a so-called limited edition for high prices. Lithographs by Miró and Chagall, for instance, were published in the French magazine *Verve* in an edition of thousands, and were also issued in "limited" editions of one hundred, numbered and signed. These numbered prints sell for much more than they would if everyone knew that they were merely part of the same practically unlimited edition.

In an extreme case, a London gallery cut color lithographs by Chagall out of *Verve* and stamped on them the signature of Chagall and a false indication that the edition was limited to two hundred.

Artists' signatures are sometimes added long after publication. Prints, originally unsigned, either because they did not meet with the artist's approval or because they appeared in a book, magazine, or other unlimited edition, often turn up with the added signature of the artist, generally forged.

Deceptive facsimiles of prints have been made, either by photomechanical means or, in the old days, by copyist-engravers working on exact-size plates or blocks. In general, such forgeries are no great problem for the collector or connoisseur, since most of the copies of the old masters have been carefully listed and described. In fact, as far as collecting old masters is concerned, prints have a great advantage over other mediums, such as drawings or paintings, because the graphic work of most of the important masters has been catalogued in detail, including notices of copies and forgeries. The authenticity of an old master print is therefore not based on the unverified opinion of a single expert. It is only in the contemporary field that extensive documentation is lacking. And the Print Council is gathering data on forgeries, reproductions, and other dubious examples with the intention of issuing a compendium of use to collectors.

In view of all the ambiguities of the art market, how can the collector be guided and protected against fraud? The best protection is education. Exposure to prints not only increases one's connoisseurship and enjoyment of prints, but is a pleasurable occupation in itself. It is possible to study unquestioned and authentic examples of prints of all schools in the print rooms of most museums, and even to obtain advice and counsel from their curators. Reading about prints helps, too; and a short bibliography of introductory works on the history and appreciation of prints has been included in the previous section. Not everybody, however, has the time or opportunity to become a print expert. The next best thing is to buy only from dealers who are known to be honorable and well informed. The collector can learn much from dealers, for it is their business to keep him interested. One should be able to obtain, if necessary, a written representation from the dealer describing the print in detail. Most honorable dealers are prepared to guarantee the authenticity of the prints they sell, and will take back a print if it is proved not to be genuine. The extent to which a dealer follows the recommendations of the Code of Dealers' Standards, outlined in Chapter VI, is a fair index of his reliability.

III

The Historical Background
of Originality

THE CONCEPT of originality in prints and the value placed upon it have undergone many changes during the centuries since prints were first made. One must distinguish between several kinds of originality, a confusion partially due to the nature of the graphic processes. One meaning relates to the artist and his work. The original artist is the creator, prime mover, inventor, as contrasted with the copyist or follower: Rembrandt as against Ferdinand Bol, or the *Apostle St. John* engraved by the Master ES as against the copy of the same subject by Israhel Van Meckenem. Two other uses of the word *original* are peculiar to printmaking, and have been discussed in the previous chapter.

Today we are much more conscious of originality in all senses of the word than our forefathers were. In the late Middle Ages when prints began to be made in Europe, the idea of originality did not exist; there were traditional themes and traditional modes of depicting them that were transmitted from artist to artist and generation to generation. Artists copied and recopied each other's work without any sense of guilt. In the medieval, and to a large extent in the Oriental conception of art, the artist's personality was submerged in his work. Pictures were not signed. The earliest signatures on prints were marks or monograms such as E S or M S (Master E S or Martin Schongauer); and it has been suggested that these marks—following the practice of goldsmiths—were hallmarks or guarantees of honest and masterly workmanship rather than signatures in the modern sense of the word. Gradually, however, as prints and easel paintings became transportable, and therefore acquired use and value as personal property, the artist's name became a valuable asset; and his production, issued under his own trademark, became almost a special brand of merchandise. Beginning at the time of the Renaissance, anonymity was replaced by the emphasis and exploitation of the artist's individual personality. The concept of plagiarism and forgery came about very gradually as a controversial issue. When Dürer went to Venice in 1505 to protest Marcantonio Raimondi's wholesale plagiarism of his *Life of the Virgin* series and other prints, the only satisfaction he could obtain from the authorities was that Raimondi was enjoined from using Dürer's monogram. In the seventeenth century artists occasionally received protection against fraudulent copying as a special favor from ruling monarchs. On certain prints published by Rubens, for example, are engraved the words *cum privilegiis regis* . . . (with the privileges or protection of the king). The first general copyright law was passed by the British Parliament in 1735 upon petition of Hogarth and others who had suffered from plagiarism and piracy. Thereafter, Hogarth's engravings—the series *Rake's Progress*, for example—bear the line *Published according to Act of Parliament*. Since then, the artist's rights in his own design have been fairly well established in most countries, in principle at least.

Again, today, we are more conscious of execution, the artist's personal touch, than were earlier print amateurs. They were more apt to value the print not for its own sake but as a surrogate of a drawing or painting. They were more concerned with a generalized outline of the composition as suggestive of sublime and noble design. They accepted the reproductive limitation of the print and did not demand the personal touch of the designer's hand. It must be remembered that the chief function of printmaking throughout its early history was reproductive. The "original" print, as we value it today, by Rembrandt, Goya, Degas, Mantegna, for example, was the exception rather than the rule. A striking example of this attitude may be seen in Van Dyck's *Iconography*. Of the hundred-odd designs that Van Dyck made for his gallery of famous men, only five of the eighteen he actually etched remained intact. The other thirteen were "finished," and all the rest completely engraved by professional craftsmen after his drawings. He had intended to do the whole set himself, but had abandoned the idea because his own presentation was unpopular. Today we are extravagant in our appraisal of his original etchings, in comparison with the rest of the *Iconography*.

It was in the nineteenth century that the concept of the original print began to emerge in tangible form. The invention of photography early in the century was a critical point in the history of printmaking, but its full impact was not realized until the end of the century, when its applications to photomechanical reproduction were perfected. The effect was revolutionary and far-reaching. As was said in *Six Centuries of Fine Prints* (New York, 1937): "Through the development of photoengraving, the line cut and the halftone, it [photography] stripped regular printmaking completely of its reproductive function. . . . The artist who now makes prints speaks not as a copyist but as a creative artist working directly in a graphic medium. This has necessitated a new orientation, a new justification for prints. They must stand or fall as an independent art."

There were also active spokesmen on behalf of the original print from about the middle of the nineteenth century onward. Whistler preached the gospel by precept and example. Seymour Haden wrote a pamphlet in 1883, *The Relative Claims of Etching and Engraving to Rank as Fine Arts,* in which he used the phrase *painter-etchers* and *painter-engravers* as opposed to reproductive craftsmen. For the purpose of his argument he classified all the creative virtues under the heading of etching and all the dull mechanical practices under the head of engraving: "The essential differences between etching and engraving may, therefore, be described as of two kinds—differences of principle, and differences of technique —and these again be expressed, not inaptly, by some such formula as the following: 'Etching, depending on brain impulse, is personal; and the creative faculty being chiefly engaged in it, invention, sensibility, and the various attributes which make up the sum of genius, belong to it and constitute it an *art.* Engraving being without personality—except such as may be supposed to be involved in the act of copying or translating the work of another—originality, and all the attributes which attend the exercise of the creative faculty, are absent from it, and constitute it a *métier.'* " The question of originals versus photomechanical reproductions also came up later in the nineteenth century. Sir Hubert Herkomer was sharply criticized in the British press by Walter Sickert and Joseph Pennell for selling photogravures of his paintings as original etchings. The influence of Whistler and Haden bore fruit in England and America in the high regard placed upon original etching at the beginning of the twentieth century. In spite of the fact that this appreciation was limited to etching (and, as it has turned out, often to etchings by artists of mediocre potential) it was a step toward the recognition of printmaking as a major medium. In France, although many of their great artists have made original prints in one form or another, there is still a large body of opinion that has no high regard for printmaking as a creative medium, and considers it a reproductive process for the luxury trade. Even after the photomechanical reproductive processes were fully perfected, "deluxe" publications were issued containing reproductions of paintings etched by mediocre artists or professional printers, designed to have a luxury or snob appeal (including such eye-catchers as Japan vellum paper, marginal *remarques*, limited editions, and fancy bindings), although in reality these "handmade" productions were inferior—as far as fidelity to the original paintings were concerned—to regular process prints. This fact and the presence of highly skilled craftsmen in printing and color work have brought about some of the questionable practices in vogue today in France.

Printmakers in America, more than in any other country today, feel an obligation to perform every step in the production of a print from the preparation of the plates, blocks, or stones to the printing of the finished impressions. This may be due in part to a dearth of skilled professional printers, who might relieve the artist of part of the burden, and in part to a sense of dedication on the part of the artist to what he considers a major creative medium, and which impels him to participate in every step of it.

In our era, then, the graphic artists—particularly Hayter and the Americans—tend to view printmaking as a major medium; and this point of view, which has also spread among critics, museum people, and the buying public, has tended to glorify originality and creation. It may be that too high a premium is being placed upon these values in the light of graphic tradition. There is an originality of design (which can still appear, although diluted, in reproductions), and there is an originality of execution (upon which the modern artists set great store). Perhaps the distinction can be made clearer by reference to another art, literature in translation. There are numerous works—often very great masterpieces—which do not suffer much by translation into a foreign tongue. Their outstanding qualities—the originality of invention, the grandeur and universality of theme, the powerful articulation of structure, the profound implications of meaning—can be carried over into another medium without too much loss of emotive power. Again, there are other works, some poems, for example, that are so idiosyncratic in expression that they can never be translated. So it is with prints. One might consider the reproductive engravings of old as translations of pictures into another medium. A translation implies a translator, who may be either pedestrian or inspired (as was Raimondi at his best). An artist can sometimes translate his own work, as in the example of Manet's *Olympia*. When Emile Zola wrote his pamphlet in defense of Manet's much criticized painting *Olympia*, and it seemed desirable to include an illustration, Manet himself made an etching of it. It was not a reproduction of the painting, though it served as one. It was actually a translation of the subject into another medium, a variant of the artist's conception. We are grateful for the occasion that induced Manet to make an original etching, designed and executed by himself. Today such a pamphlet would probably be illustrated with a process color reproduction.

If engravings are translations, then photomechanical prints might be called reproductions, pure and simple. The personality of the translator, with all its advantages and disadvantages, does not intervene. The original artists' prints of today might be called poems that cannot be translated into a foreign tongue.

[24]

The practice of signing prints in pencil or ink is of fairly recent origin. The earliest prints were not signed at all. Later a signature or monogram was placed directly on the plate, block, or stone, either in the composition or in the margin directly below. Most reproductive prints, logically, have notations in the margin indicating the painter and engraver; for instance, on the *Village Dance* is engraved on the left *Rubens pinx.* (Rubens painted it) and on the right *Bolswert sculp.* (Bolswert engraved it). Whistler and Haden were among the first to sign their prints in pencil. Whistler's later prints were signed with his Butterfly mark and the letters *imp.*, indicating that he also printed the plate. Whistler's and Haden's earlier prints were issued unsigned. The theoretical justification for the artist's signature in pencil is the implication that he inspected the impression and approved of it. It is amusing to note that Haden would sign any early unsigned print brought to him for the fee of a guinea. The later British and American schools, D. Y. Cameron, Muirhead Bone, John Taylor Arms, and the like, were quite meticulous in the printing and signing of their proofs. Today practically all prints are signed in pencil by the artist, and the signature is assumed to be a guarantee of authenticity and originality.

In the matter of limiting editions of prints, current practice differs markedly from that of the past. In the old days plates were not destroyed, but were printed from until they wore out or were reworked beyond recognition. How many of such prints were good? We rarely have actual data. Adam Bartsch, himself a competent printmaker, furnished, in his learned *Anleitung zur Kupferstichkunde*, in 1821, some figures as to the quantity that can be produced by various mediums. A copper engraving, according to him, can yield about 500 good prints and 500 weaker ones; stipple engraving likewise 500 good and 500 weaker ones; a mezzotint about 300 to 400, of which the first 150 are good; aquatint on copper less than 200; a drypoint not more than 150 impressions of diverse quality. A wood block, according to whether it is lightly or deeply cut, is good for from 8,000 to 10,000 impressions. Some of the wood engraving blocks from Thomas Bewick's *Birds* and *Quadrupeds* are still in existence. Recently some impressions were taken from them, printed with care and expertness. It is astonishing how well the blocks have stood up under the pressure and strain of printing the many editions of the blocks. In the opinion of many who have seen them, the late impressions are superior to the earlier ones because at last they are properly printed. Bartsch, at the time of writing, had no experience with lithography, but other authorities have given figures from 800 to 1,000 from a stone, and more with transfers. It is known that of one of the Currier and Ives lithographs, 73,000 prints were sold.

An invention of the mid-nineteenth century also has some bearing on printing quality and limitation, namely, steel-facing, which can practically eliminate wear and tear on a copperplate. In spite of the authority of such experts as Maxime Lalanne, Félix Bracquemond, S. R. Koehler, Seymour Haden, Frederick Goulding, Philip Hamerton, Sir Frank Short, and David Strang, there still seems to be a great deal of misunderstanding, even prejudice, regarding steel-facing. Sir Frank Short has made the statement that it is exceedingly difficult, if not impossible, even for an artist or printer, to tell the difference between proofs from the coated and uncoated copper, provided equal care is exercised in the printing of both. There even have been successful experiments in printing a copperplate, half of which was steel-faced. The reason steel-faced prints have acquired a bad name is that they have often been printed in a slipshod manner. It may, therefore, be accepted that steel-facing does not appreciably impair the printing quality of a plate, and does prevent it from wearing down. David Strang, in his authoritative book *The Printing of Etchings and Engravings,* cites the theoretical case of a drypoint copperplate capable of yielding thirty impressions, each proof becoming progressively weaker with the printing of each impression. He calculates that the difference in effect between the original copper surface and the steel-facing would be equivalent to the effect produced by the printing of one to three trial proofs from the bare copper. If therefore the plate were immediately steel-faced and an edition of thirty proofs run off, each proof would be the equivalent in quality, one might say, to the third proof from the bare copper. If, on the other hand, the whole edition were printed from the original copper, there might be two proofs superior to the steel-face proof, but there would be twenty-seven that would be inferior.

Nowadays only small editions of prints are made. In the United States, editions of 10 to 15 are frequent, from 35 to 50 common, seldom as many as 75 to 100 impressions. In Europe, editions by popular artists may run up to 200 or 250, but average runs are much less. In the Soviet Union and other Communist countries, the editions may be higher. In general, however, the number printed does not reflect the full yield possible. Granted that Bartsch was very generous in his estimates and not too fastidious as to the printing quality, granted that copper was harder in the past (that is, beaten instead of rolled) and that there is a prejudice against steel-facing, there still remains an enormous gap between actual and potential yield in current practice. The limitation is arbitrary, and has been imputed to commercial motives. Sir Francis Seymour Haden was against artificial limitation, and has been quoted as having besought the Society of Painter-Etchers, whose first president he became in 1890, never to adopt that commercial method. One doubts that all contemporary printmakers are really so mercenary. It is more likely that they are unwilling to spend too much time in printing their works and that, in general, distribution methods have not kept up with the enormous increase in production. In the overall picture, however, it is ironic that in an era when there are more and more practicing printmakers and more and more potential customers for their work, there should be a definite trend toward artificial limitation.

In the past there was a division of labor in the production of prints. The earliest woodcuts were the product of two sets of hands, the designer and the woodcutter, or *Formschneider*. In the sixteenth century the names of the designers generally became known, whereas the woodcutters usually remained anonymous but often highly skilled craftsmen. We do, however, know the names of several, such as Lützelberger, who cut Holbein's *Dance of Death*, and Boldrini, who cut blocks for Titian. Dürer did not cut all his own wood blocks, although he engraved all his own copper engravings. We do not think the less of Dürer's woodcuts or those of Cranach because they were cut by other hands. Among Chinese and Japanese prints, likewise, there was a division of labor between the designer, the woodcutter, and the printer; and the finest Japanese prints are held in high esteem. Here and today, the artists cut and print their own blocks; and even in Japan there is a new kind of original print, *Sōsaku Hanga*, following the example of the West in uniting the functions of the designer, cutter, and printer. It has happened occasionally that electrotypes have been made directly from a wood block and that prints were then taken from the metal plate instead of from the wood, as for instance with some of the reproductive wood engravings of Timothy Cole. Although it would be extremely difficult to distinguish, on visual evidence alone, between prints from the two sources, purists claim that only those from wood are entitled to rank as true prints.

In the early days engravings or etchings were probably

printed in the artists' studios (Dürer's or Rembrandt's, for example) by pupils and apprentices. Later, professional plate printers appeared: Bosse has a picture of such a studio. Some of the nineteenth-century printers—Eugène Delâtre or Frederick Goulding—were renowned for the beauty and expertness of their printing. We do not value a fine etching by Charles Méryon the less for having been printed by Delâtre. The technical treatment was relatively uncomplicated, and the effect was dependent on straightforward drawing and subtle biting. A sensitive printer, given a model to follow, could produce any number of beautiful impressions up to the limit of the life of the copperplate. When, however, the plate became worn with repeated printings, and was reworked and reinforced by foreign hands, the quality of the impressions deteriorated, as the sad specimens of late Rembrandts, Van Dycks, Piranesis, Goyas, and other *chalcographie* prints can plainly bear witness. Nonetheless, this negative judgment refers chiefly to the quality of the impression: such prints are still original prints, although pale reflections of fine early examples. Fraud enters into the situation only where someone, trading on the name and fame of the artist, misrepresents the quality of late impressions for commercial gain. The cultivated amateur or collector is much more conscious of printing quality today than in the past. If this were not true, then the various *chalcographies* of Rome, Paris, and Madrid would never have come into being.

The professional printer has been more consistently employed in lithography than in the other graphic mediums. Even today relatively few artists print their own lithographs. This may be due partly to the fact that a lithographic press is cumbersome and would occupy a large space in an artist's studio, but chiefly to the fact that quality in printing is dependent upon manual manipulation and intangibles of long experience. One cannot learn much about lithographic printing from a technical manual. Therefore, throughout the history of lithography, prints have been considered originals and in fact great masterpieces, even though they were not printed by the artist—Goya's *Bullfights,* for example, or the lithographs of Toulouse-Lautrec.

In making a lithograph it is possible for an artist to draw not only on stone or a metal plate but also on a piece of paper from which the design can be transferred to the stone by a skilled printer. The practice of transfer printing dates back to Senefelder's example, but some purists claim that prints made by this method are not originals but reproductions. The issue was settled once for all in a celebrated libel suit, instituted by Pennell and Whistler against Walter Sickert in 1897 in reply to an article in the *Saturday Review.* Sickert had argued that to pass off drawings on paper as lithographs was misleading "to the purchaser on the vital point of commercial value." After a parade of distinguished witnesses and the citation of historical evidence, a verdict was found against Sickert, and transfer lithographs were established as legitimate original prints. Usually the artist, after the transfer has been made, continues to work on the stone. One use of the transfer does lead to questionable practices, namely, when the finished drawing on a stone is transferred to another stone solely for the purpose of making a large edition. Some of Whistler's lithographs appeared in publications—*The Studio, The Albermarle, The Art Journal,* for example. Whistler's original drawing on stone was transferred to other stones for the production of the necessarily large editions. Whatever quality the hand proofs might have had vanished in the mechanical printing; and such prints on mediocre paper might be called reproductions, although in a broad interpretation they could still pass as originals.

If the facts of retransfer are known, the authenticity might be questionable, since the artist did not actually work on each retransfer of the original master image. But if the case history of the printing is not known—as in most cases it is not—the print might have to be accepted on its face value as an original. There have been instances, however, where a lithograph stone has been prepared for printing from a rare lithographic print, not by direct transfer from the original print at the time it was made, but much later by photographing the print on the stone in exact size. The prints made from such a stone are, of course, deliberate forgeries.

The technique known as offset lithographic printing poses a special problem. The design is not printed from the stone or plate directly, but from a rubber blanket that has picked up the inked image from the lithograph plate attached to a cylinder—a double printing, as it were. It is a process that eliminates rolling up by hand in the interests of speed and quantity printing. It is therefore a borderline case more slanted toward reproductive than toward original production. But occasionally an artist (Jean Charlot, for example) has drawn lithographs with this process definitely in mind, and has thereby created charming and effective original prints. The offset principle (not necessarily lithographic) has also been used in combination with other mediums (by S. W. Hayter and others) to add touches of color to color prints.

The silk-screen stencil medium has been adapted for artists' use within the last twenty-five years. A number of artists who make original prints in the medium have decided to call them *serigraphs* to distinguish them from commercial silk-screen reproductions. The process has also been used in conjunction with other mediums for the production of original color prints.

There are cases where a print was only partially executed by the artist, with assistance from other sources. May such works be classified as original prints? Corot, being primarily a painter and not a professional etcher, had trouble with the biting of his plates. In the etching *Souvenir d'Italie*, his friend Bracquemond performed that service for him, no doubt with the collaboration of the artist, who, of course, drew the design on the copper. Such an etching is usually considered an original print. When Georges Rouault was working on his series *Miserere*, photogravure plates were made of the preliminary drawings. These plates were then reworked with burin, drypoint, acquatint, and the like, by the artist himself. Since the photomechanical work was transformed or incorporated in the artist's own handling, the finished product may properly be regarded as an original print. Cézanne, who likewise was primarily a painter and not a professional printmaker, drew a composition, *Bathers*, on a stone. From a trial proof colored by Cézanne in watercolor, the printer made color separations and prepared stones for further printing to produce the color lithograph. This print, greatly esteemed by collectors, may be rated as more than half original, since the supplementary work was done under the artist's supervision, and was based on a model made expressly for the purpose.

In conclusion, one may summarize the problem of reproductive versus original prints somewhat as follows: Owing to the impact of photography and photomechanical processes, a new attitude toward printmaking has developed that stresses the original, the creative factor. In general, one may say that handwork is bound up with art and original execution, as opposed to automation and mechanical processes.

In past print history, the invention per se, the design and the message, were what the public looked for and prized. To be sure, the original artist of old also was concerned with the execution and with the effort to clothe his conception in the most perfect form possible. But that concern was his private affair, related to his artistic conscience, and of interest, possibly, only to his fellow practitioners, but certainly not to the layman in general. The modern artists (and through them now the public at large) tend to be conscious not only of what they say but also of how they say it. Indeed, they almost make the latter the prime creative motivation. Thus, when they make a print, they maintain that it is a complete aesthetic entity, a perfect fusion of concept and form, a work of art that could not exist in any other shape or form and that is fully the equal in validity and impact of an oil painting, irrespective of whether it exists in one or more impressions. But in any estimate of rank between major and minor art, one must remember that printmaking really cannot count on the still potent asset of uniqueness, as can painting, drawing, and, to a lesser extent, plastic art (which also has its problem with casts as multi-originals). The transvaluation of printmaking from minor into major, however, is in the spirit of the age, and must be reckoned with.

It is imperative above all that we come to terms with certain attitudes—holdovers from the past—which, being less scrupulous in discrimination between original and reproductive, are causing confusion and misunderstanding. These notes are designed to review objectively the conflicting standards of business morality held by some artists and some dealers. It may turn out that the problem is one of semantics rather than ethics. We must make the issue widespread and make clear just what the difference is between original and reproductive. These notes also aim to place this very modern problem into some sort of historical perspective in order to serve as a corrective of any uninformed criticism from the modern point of view of various practices in the past. These procedures might be deemed questionable today, whereas they were quite legitimate in the framework of their time. One can be rigid in applying certain standards to the works of our time, but one may not to those of the past.

So much for the original print in the past. What about its status in the future? There is of course no absolute assurance that the criteria of the past or even of the present will continue to be accepted unchanged and unchallenged in the future. There are already some faint signs that a transvaluation of values may be in the making. The present concept of the original print represents the climax and apotheosis of individuality. The ideal of the established artists of our day, and particularly of the printmakers, is idiosyncrasy of expression, the artist's personal touch. The artist has his own message, which he expresses in his own inimitable way, performing each step toward the ultimate end with his own hand and eye. A public, having grown to like and admire his productions, has placed a cachet of value upon his expression because of its personal and technical idiosyncrasy. But the continued ascendancy of such a concept is by no means secure. Young artists and new movements are emerging, and will continue to emerge, to vie with the older artists and win their own following. The names of the movements are irrelevant—they succeed each other in bewildering profusion, and here is not the place to present a history of modern "isms"— the movements are significant only insofar as they indicate a trend, a growing indifference to means and techniques.

Many of the artists of the *avant-garde* are inclined to reject traditions of the past, particularly the tradition of handwork in the production of prints. They tend to concentrate their efforts on the invention and perfection of their personal "gimmick," which distinguishes them from other competing artists. When they seek a wider audience through the production and distribution of prints, they are apt to be impatient of the "drudgery" involved, and fall back upon the impersonality of the photomechanical processes, which interpose the least possible barrier between the original and its multiplication. Why use cumbersome and antiquated methods, when easy modern methods are at hand? In many cases the artists may not even know that other methods exist, for they make a point of ignoring the past. Nor would the public that collects their work by fad or inclination care one way or another how their prints were made: it will accept anything from a successful artist.

As a matter of fact, the public is becoming more and more accustomed to impersonal mass production in every branch of life. "Mass-Man" would not balk at mass-produced images. It could happen, therefore, that the word *original* might lose its special meaning, and the distinction between original and reproduction, or between art (as we know it now) and non-art might lose its force. No one would care about the ethics or semantics involved. Such suppositions are of course pure speculation. Nonetheless they remain a possibility. If the tradition of the original print and its production were forgotten, let us hope that some new word would be found for the new form that would take its place, and that the old words *original prints* would still be reserved to describe the masterpieces of our own age.

IV

Glossary of Terms Relating to Prints

1. TECHNIQUES OF PRINTMAKING

The compiler is indebted to many sources, but especially to Hans W. Singer's *Die Fachaus-drücke der Graphik*, and Felix Brunner's *Handbook of Graphic Reproduction Processes*. In recent years there has been a proliferation of new materials and techniques of printmaking. The glossary below does not attempt to include every up-to-the-minute method, but is limited largely to those in use for about a decade.

AQUATINT (*aquatinte, Aquatinta*). An intaglio method for producing more or less uniform tones on an etched plate of copper or zinc. The artist dusts powdered rosin (colophony, or *Kolophonium* in German, a turpentine derivative) on the plate through a cloth bag or in a specially designed dustbox. When the plate is warmed, the particles adhere to it and create minute areas of exposed copper of characteristic pattern or grain. The grain may be fine or coarse, depending upon whether fine or coarse particles of rosin are used. The plate is placed in an acid bath that eats into the exposed areas of metal. The design on the plate is developed and the gradations of tone are achieved by repeated bitings of the plate. In the first rebiting, all the areas intended to be in the lightest tone are "stopped out" or covered with an acid-resisting varnish, and the plate is again immersed in the acid bath. The process is repeated until the scale of tones from light to dark is laid down, the areas of darkest tone being those that are bitten the longest and deepest.

The plate is printed as one would print any intaglio plate. Although prints have been made in pure aquatint (by Goya, for example), the medium has generally been combined with regular or soft-ground etching to produce both linear and tonal elements on the same plate. Instead of the dusting method, aquatint can be laid with a liquid ground of rosin dissolved in spirits of wine (a variety of alcohol). When the alcohol evaporates, the rosin dries with a characteristic crackle. An approximation to aquatint may be made by pressing sandpaper on a plate covered with a regular hard ground. If the sandpaper and plate are run through a press several times, the sand particles will pierce the hard ground to produce a multitude of tiny holes. The plate can then be treated in the regular way. The grain can be varied by using sandpapers of varying fineness. This method is known as sandpaper aquatint. To recognize aquatint in general on a print, examine it with a magnifying glass. You will soon learn to distinguish the characteristic grain, sometimes with a minute crackle effect, similar to old porcelain. The prints will also have the typical plate mark of intaglio printing.

CARBOGRAPH. A variant of mezzotint, perfected around 1939 in the Pennsylvania Art Project by Dox Thrash, Michael Gallagher, and Hubert Mesibov. The metal is scratched with carborundum crystals and a levigator, producing a fair approximation of a mezzotint ground with much less labor and time. The creation of the design and the printing proceeds as with regular mezzotint.

CELLOCUT. Perfected by Boris Margo. Any smooth surface, of metal or plywood, for example, may be coated and built up with a liquid type of plastic, such as celluloid dissolved in acetone. When it has set, the resulting surface may be worked with either woodcut or intaglio tools. The plates are printed either in intaglio or in relief in an etching press. See also RELIEF PROCESSES.

CHIAROSCURO WOODCUT (*gravure en camaïeu, clair-obscur, Helldunkelholzschnitt*). A type of woodcut, printed in color, perfected in the early sixteenth century. It was probably first made in imitation of chiaroscuro drawings in which the design is drawn in black on toned or colored paper, and the highlights are touched in with white pigment. Giorgio Vasari wrongly credited Ugo da Carpi with its invention: both Hans Burgkmair and Lucas Cranch produced chiaroscuro prints before him. This form of color printing involves the use of several blocks, a key block and one or more tone blocks, out of which certain areas have been cut to allow the blank paper to show through and produce the effect of highlights.

CLICHÉ VERRE (French term, but also much used in English). A drawing is made on a glass plate coated with a dark emulsion. Wherever the stylus makes a line through the coating, it is exposed as transparent glass. A facsimile of the drawing can be produced on photographic paper by exposure to light and development in the usual way. It is a simple primitive duplicating medium, but it is not based upon the principle or aim of photography, which is the translation of an image of natural objects to a plate in terms of light and dark. It is an autographic process, although it has borrowed some technical steps from photography. Corot and Millet were the most famous practitioners of the art at the time when it was first perfected.

COLLOGRAPH. See RELIEF PROCESSES.

COLOR PRINTING. The earliest attempts at color printing were made during the last quarter of the fifteenth century. In 1485, Erhard Ratdolt, in Venice, printed astronomical diagrams in red, orange, and black from wood blocks. All graphic mediums have been employed in the making of color prints. In general, a separate block or plate is prepared for each color, and the final composition built up by successive printings. In theory the idea is simple, but in practice very expert technical manipulation is called for. Great care must be exercised to make sure that the paper is always in contact with the plate in exactly the same place. Otherwise, there will be gaps or overlappings in the color pattern—a defect known as being "off register." Since the printer works blind, that is to say, he lays the paper face down upon the plate for each successive step in color printing, it is obvious that the task is not easy. Various devices have been used to overcome the difficulty. One of the commonest is to bore tiny holes in the two corners of the plate or in the margin of the stone, fix pins in them, and fit them through holes in the paper properly placed. When dampened paper is used in printing (intaglio, for instance), a further complication arises from the fact that paper, as it is dampened and dried, does not always return to its exact size, but stretches in one dimension or another, thus throwing the register marks askew. Color prints can also be made from a single block or plate by successive ink-ings and printings, where color areas are far enough apart to ink them in different colors, or in a single print from a mezzotint plate, for example, by inking in the colors with daubers of colored inks (*à la poupée*), painting the plate, as it were, in one operation. Much more can be said about color printing—in fact, books have been written on the subject—

but enough has been said to demonstrate that color printing is a complicated process and an impressive technical achievement.

CRAYON MANNER. See STIPPLE PRINT.

DOTTED PRINT. See METAL CUT.

DRYPOINT (*pointe sèche, Kaltnadel*). An intaglio variant of engraving. The linear design is scratched on a copper or zinc plate with a hard steel or diamond point. The action of the point, unlike that of a burin, forces the metal up on one or both sides of the furrow, depending upon the angle of inclination. The metal projections called the burr (*barbe, Grat*) are not removed—again unlike the practice of engraving, where the metal shavings are removed with a scraper—but furnish, when the plate is inked and printed, the characteristic velvety black of the drypoint line. A plate with much burr on it cannot be wiped as clean for printing as an engraved plate because the burr retains the ink; by the same token, a drypoint plate wears down very quickly because the burr is vulnerable to the action of wiping and the pressure of the press. To overcome the handicap of rapid wear, a process known as steel-facing (*acierage, Verstählung*) is employed. A minute coating of hard iron is laid on the metal plate by electrolytic means; the facing does not affect the quality of printing to any appreciable degree (see Chapter III, "The Historical Background of Originality," for a further discussion of the problem), but it does preserve the plate from wear. Drypoint lines are sometimes added to etched plates for additional color and variety (as Rembrandt did, for example). Drypoint has been used as early as Dürer's time. In general it can be said that drypoints are the easiest to draw on the plate, but the hardest to print.

ELECTRON PRINT. In electron prints, as developed by Caroline Durieux with the technical aid of Professor Harry E. Wheeler at Louisiana State University, a radioactive isotope (radioactive forms of elements, such as carbon, sulfur, calcium, and the like) is mixed with a dye ink (Higgins Eterna); the artist uses the resultant mixture to make a drawing with a pen or brush. A sheet of sensitized paper is placed in direct contact with the drawing when dry; and the radioactive particles reconstruct the image on the paper, which is then developed and fixed as in a regular photographic print. The process can be repeated indefinitely during the effective life of the isotope. The result is an extraordinarily faithful replica of the drawing in reverse. It is a true print, and not a photomechanical reproduction or a reproductive photograph. It differs from a photomechanical reproduction because the transmission is direct and without any mechanical intervention. It is not a photograph because the image is not produced by the action of reflected light upon certain chemical substances on a plate. Electron prints are not reflections of external appearance, but have a direct and intimate connection with the artist's own handiwork.

EMBOSSED PRINT (*glyptographie, cérographie, stéréotype, gauffrure, gauffrage, Blinddruck, Blindpressung*). Those which contain areas of three-dimensional form, that is to say, areas either projecting above or depressed below the surface of the paper. The paper is generally of unusual thickness and strength to retain the impressed forms. Embossing was first used systematically by Elisha Kirkall in 1722–1724, and Arthur Pond in 1732–1736. The Japanese began embossing around 1730. Harunobu and, later, Utamaro used it skillfully to produce areas of varying texture. In the epoch of *Art Nouveau* in France, compositions modeled in low relief by sculptors were stamped out in heavy paper, under the name of *stéréotypes, cérographies*, or *glyptographies*. In recent times American printmakers have experimented with the plastic effects possible in so traditionally two-dimensional a medium as the print. Most of such prints are abstract in style, some with touches of color, but many are conceived in terms of pure form, white on white. The effects are achieved by overlays of metal or leather on a plate, producing concave or hollow areas; or by gouging into the surface of the plate to produce convex or protuberant surfaces on the paper. Rolf Nesch has also produced plastic effects in his metal prints. See METAL PRINT.

ENCAUSTIC COLOR PRINTING. A method invented by Milton Goldstein for printing with wax or encaustic crayons instead of color inks. The crayons are rubbed on the etched or aquatinted plate, and can be blended. The plate is warmed to fuse the colors, and printed in the usual way, but generally with an overlay by relief printing to harmonize the colors.

ENGRAVING, LINE (*gravure en taille douce, gravure au trait, gravure sur cuivre, Linienstich, Kupferstich, Grabstichelarbeit*). The earliest of the intaglio processes, dating from the first half of the fifteenth century. The design is incised in a copperplate with a tool called a graver or a burin (*burin, Grabstichel*). The deeper the sharp lozenge-shaped end of the burin digs into the metal, the wider the line. The sharply pointed cut produced as the graver enters the copper and again comes out of the furrow is one of the distinguishing marks of the engraved line. When an engraved line in a print is examined with a magnifying glass, the pointed ends are clearly visible in contradistinction to the blunter ends of an etched line. Engraving is a laborious and time-consuming process, and was much employed by the reproductive engravers of the seventeenth to the mid-nineteenth centuries. It has recently been revived as a creative medium by Stanley William Hayter and his school. The printing of engravings follows the general pattern of intaglio printing (see below).

EPOXY PRINTS. See RELIEF PROCESSES.

ETCHING (*eau forte, Radierung*). An intaglio linear process, perfected in Germany during the first quarter of the sixteenth century. The earliest etchings were from iron plates, but after 1520 copperplates came into general use. Zinc plates have also been used during the last hundred years. An acid-resisting ground (a combination of wax, mastic, and asphaltum) is laid on a polished metal plate. It is applied either with a roller or a dabber on a warm plate, or poured on in liquid form. The artist draws with an etching needle through the ground, thus creating his design in lines of exposed metal. The plate is then immersed in an acid bath (nitric or other mordants), whereupon the acid attacks or "bites" into the exposed lines, producing incised lines approximating burin work without any of the hard work. Thus etching became a laborsaving device that could engrave more speedily by chemical means.

The etched line has somewhat the quality of a drawn line, quite unlike the regular system of lines produced by the tight and constrained action of the burin. This is one of the great advantages—aside from the rapidity—of the etching technique: one can actually draw on the plate, the lines moving freely in any direction. The variation in the width or depth of the line is accomplished in engraving by the degree to which the burin digs into the metal, whether deeply or shallowly. In etching it is obtained in a different way, namely, by repeated bitings of the plate. When the plate with the design on it is taken out of the first bath, the lines are discovered to be uniformly and faintly bitten. Then the artist covers over, with acid-resisting "stopping-out" varnish (*Deckwachs*), all the lines that he wishes to remain light and delicate. The plate is again put into the bath for further biting of the lines not covered by stopping-out varnish as well as by the ground. The longer the plate remains in the mordant bath, the deeper and wider the exposed lines become. The process of stopping out intermediate lines and rebiting is repeated again and again until only the heaviest lines remain exposed to the acid. In this way a great variety of line work can be obtained. Then

[44]

the ground is removed, and the plate is cleaned and ready to be printed in the usual way. (See INTAGLIO PRINTING.)

INTAGLIO MIXED METHODS. A term used to describe any complicated intaglio process or combination of processes used in the production of modern prints. Among the processes that can be or have been employed are: engraving, etching, lift-ground and regular aquatint; impresses on soft ground of various textiles, the grains of woods, leaves, pieces of string, crumpled paper, and the like; graining with carborundum and other abrasives; rubbing down with rottenstone and burnishers; welding of mesh, wire, and other metal objects to the plate; various collage operations, roulette work, punch engraving, the gouging of holes in the plate, and finally offset techniques for color areas. Mixed methods can also refer to printing processes. In color printing, the same plate can be printed intaglio for the lines and then in relief, as in a woodcut, for surface tones.

INTAGLIO PRINTING (*impression en creux, Tiefdruck*). The method of printing any incised or etched plate, in other words, the printing of etchings, engravings, aquatints, drypoints, stipples, mezzotints, and the like. The plate, ready for printing, is covered solidly with printing ink by means of a dabber or roller, making sure that the ink is forced into all the incised lines. The ink is fairly stiff, and the plate is usually warmed to make it more workable. The surplus ink is wiped off the surface of the plate by means of muslin cloths, and the final wiping done with the palm of the hand. For engravings the plate is wiped very clean and the operation finished with a little whiting on the hand. For etchings a little ink is often left on the plate, giving the print a slight tone instead of a dead white, and with a cloth the ink is drawn up slightly out of the lines in an operation known as *retroussage*. (Some artists, notably Rembrandt and Whistler, left a great deal of ink on certain plates, and, manipulating the ink adroitly, achieved extraordinary tonal effects of chiaroscuro. Such prints are practically monotypes, since the effect would vary with each printing.)

The plate, now inked and still warm, is placed face up on the bed of a roller press. A sheet of dampened paper (dampened to make it more pliable to be forced into the incised lines of the plate) is laid upon it, and upon it several blotters and blankets, and then run through the press under heavy pressure. The paper, when lifted off the plate, is found to have picked up the ink from the incised lines. The corresponding lines on the paper appear to be ever so slightly raised in relief. The damp proof is placed between blotters to dry, or better yet, tacked down on a board along the edges of the margins, in order that the print may dry flat and not be wrinkled. Printing ink (*encre, Druckfarbe*) is made by grinding lampblack (Frankfort black or French black) with a medium-burnt linseed oil (practically a varnish). The addition of burnt umber warms the black tone. Many variations and combinations are possible. A method for obtaining a proof from an intaglio plate without a press has been described by Maxime Lalanne and has been used by some modern artists. A raised wooden frame is erected around the edges of the inked plate, and liquid plaster of Paris poured into the area. When the plaster is set, it can be lifted off to serve as an inked impression of the plate. A distinguishing mark of all intaglio prints is the impression made by the plate itself on the paper, namely, the plate mark (*cuvette, Facettenrand*). It must be remembered, however, that in many old prints the plate mark is not visible because all the margins have been cut off. If the edge of the plate is sharp, it is apt to cut into the paper under the strong pressure. It is therefore common practice to file down the edges into a bevel (*biseau, Facette, Schmiege*).

INTAGLIO PROCESS (*gravure en creux, Tiefdruck*). A general term descriptive of all techniques employing the intaglio principle of duplication, where the design is incised below the surface of the plate, which may be of copper, zinc, aluminum, steel, magnesium, celluloid, Lucite, and the like. Among them may be cited the following: aquatint, carbograph, collograph, crayon manner, drypoint, embossed printing, line engraving, etching, lift-ground etching, metal printing, mezzotint, soft-ground etching, stipple engraving, sugar aquatint.

LIFT-GROUND ETCHING (*réservage, Aussprengverfahren*) is a process generally used in conjunction with aquatint, and hence is also called sugar aquatint or sugar-lift aquatint. By this process, the artist can make his design with a single stroke of the brush, in contrast to the more negative procedure of regular aquatint, where a line or area is defined by coating its boundaries with impervious stopping-out varnish. Lift-ground etching employs the so-called wash-out principle. The artist makes his design upon a plate with a brush and a viscous liquid of varying composition, among the ingredients of which are India ink or gamboge, saturated sugar solution or corn syrup, glycerin or liquid soap. When the drawing is almost dry (for it is designed not to dry completely), a coating of regular liquid etching ground is laid over the whole plate. When this is set, the plate is put in a bath of warm water. The areas covered by the drawing mixture are attacked by the water, and the covering ground is undermined to expose the bare metal in the pattern of the original drawing. An aquatint ground is laid on the exposed parts and bitten (or possibly rebitten) in the usual way. It is assumed that Gainsborough used the method in some of his landscape etchings in the eighteenth century. Picasso has used it with conspicuous success in recent times. It is also possible to use the lift-ground process without adding aquatint. Misch Kohn, for example, has allowed the viscous liquid to drip on a plate, without a brush, and created designs by calligraphic swirls and controlled or haphazard dots and spots.

LINOLEUM CUT. A variant of the woodcut, using a piece of linoleum instead of a wood block. Since it is very easy to work in linoleum, it has been much used by amateurs. Picasso, however, has raised the medium to the dignity of an art form.

LITHOGRAPHY (*lithographie, lithographe, Steindruck, Polyautographie*). A planographic process called "chemical printing" by Aloys Senefelder, who invented it around 1798. The typical procedure may be described as follows: A design is drawn with a greasy crayon on a thick slab of polished and grained limestone. Once the greasy drawing is applied to the stone, it must be "fixed," or prevented from spreading, by a chemical operation known as the "etch," a mixture of gum and nitric acid. The name "etch" is unfortunate and confusing, for it bears no resemblance to the process of etching on copper, and does not eat into the stone. Its purpose is merely to prevent the grease from spreading during the continuous rolling necessary in applying the ink.

Another point about lithography is that the artist draws more or less blindly, that is to say, without knowing the exact shade of dark he will achieve. In lithographic drawing, what is decisive is the grease content upon the stone. But because grease is colorless, lampblack is added to the crayon in order that the artist may have a rough idea of what he is doing. He must learn by experience to calculate the exact proportion of lampblack to grease in his crayon. The lampblack does not count in the final result. It is washed out with a turpentine solution in one of the most dramatic operations of the whole process. It would seem as if all the artist's labor in drawing were washed out and destroyed. But the grease is still locked in the stone, and the design appears as if by magic when the stone is inked up for the first time. Before the oily, greasy ink is applied, the stone must be thoroughly dampened with a wet sponge, for the key principle of the operation is the antipathy of grease and water. When the ink is rolled over the damp areas of the stone, it will not stick, but will be readily accepted wherever there is a greasy mark. Thus a complete facsimile of the original drawing in all its shades appears in ink on the stone, and can be transferred to a sheet of paper through a specially designed press.

Because the earliest prints made by the process were printed from stone, the technique has been called lithography, from the Greek words meaning stone writing. It is possible to use the thick stone slabs (thick, to avoid cracking under pressure) over again by grinding off the design with abrasives and a levigator, or more generally with one stone on top of another. Other materials, such as sheets of zinc or aluminum, properly grained, have been used instead of stone. Metal plates are more transportable but suffer from other disadvantages: the surface is not so pleasant to work on, and one cannot make corrections or use scratch techniques. The crayons used—and their liquid equivalent, tusche or lithographic ink—are made of a mixture of grease, wax, soap, and lampblack. But any greasy substance, including lipstick, the imprint of a human hand, or even a sneeze, will produce some effect. Many technical manipulations are possible: a range of hard to soft crayons; rubbed tones with soft crayon and chamois; scratch techniques with a razor blade, needle, sandpaper, or eraser; tusche effects with pen, brush, drybrush, or spatterwork (such as little dots spun from an old toothbrush); impresses of textiles or other objects; and washings with benzene or turpentine. It is possible to transfer (*umdrucken*) a lithographic drawing on paper (preferably a specially prepared paper) onto a stone without any appreciable loss of drawing values, and then print it in the usual way. The image, of course, will be reversed in the transfer.

[49]

Lithography is well adapted for color printing. Lithographic drawings executed in washes are sometimes called lithotints. Lithographic printing inks have a little more grease content than other inks, but must be strong and fairly stiff; otherwise the stone will smear. A lithographic crayon line, when magnified, is revealed as a series of minute dots determined by the grain of the stone. They can be distinguished from the somewhat similar dots of soft-ground etching, for example, because they do not have the slightly raised surface characteristic of intaglio printing. Soft-ground etching has a plate mark, but so does a lithograph printed from zinc, except when the paper is the same size as the plate. There is one distinguishing sign of a lithograph printed from stone, which is visible when looking at a proof from a raking angle: It will be seen that the surface of the paper is smoother and more polished wherever it has passed between the scraper and the stone. The outline of the stone is thus faintly visible.

MANIÈRE CRIBLÉE. See METAL CUT.

METAL CUT (*Metalschnitt*). A name applied to certain old engravings printed from metal plates but printed, like a wood block, in relief. The name "relief print" has also been used. Among such examples may be cited the illustrations in the French-printed Books of Hours around 1500, and those early prints known as dotted prints (*manière criblée, Schrotblatt*), made with various goldsmith's punches on metal.

METAL PRINT (*Metaldruck*). An intaglio process perfected by Rolf Nesch. He attached wire, pieces of mesh or metal, flat washers, and other *objets trouvés* to his copperplates as part of the design, and ran them through the press, either inked or uninked, to produce unique plastic effects. Nesch was also the first to make holes in his plates for aesthetic purposes. His first experiment in this direction is dated 1925.

MEZZOTINT (*manière noire, Schabkunst*). An intaglio

tone process. A German soldier named Ludwig von Siegen is credited with its invention. (His first dated print is 1643.) But the improvements by Abraham Blooteling later in the century proved more decisive in the practice of the craft. Siegen obtained his tonal areas by rolling every whichway with a spur-like instrument that later developed into the roulette, or tiny wheel with teeth. The more one rolled, the darker the area would print, and so he worked from light to dark. Blooteling invented a more efficient instrument for graining, called a rocker, and with it laid a mezzotint ground over the whole plate. The plate was entirely and evenly pitted and roughened with tiny holes. If the plate were printed in this state, it would print solid black. Then, working from dark to light, he would work over a certain area with a scraper and burnisher, flattening and pressing the copper, and erasing the holes, as it were, and making the surface smooth again, so that it would not hold ink, and therefore print white. The mezzotint process, based upon gradations of tones, was particularly suited to reproduce paintings, and was so employed. A mezzotint plate is printed in the same way as all intaglios, and particularly as a drypoint plate, the burr of which has a slight similarity to the pits and indentations of the mezzotint plate.

MONOTYPE. By definition and etymology, a monotype is a print printed in only one impression, and therefore hardly fits into the category of multi-original printmaking. It is more truly a drawing with printed features. The process is simple: A plate on which a design has been painted is covered with a sheet of paper and run through a press. The design is transferred to the paper as a monotype. The plate may be copper or other metal or even glass. The pigment, either monochrome or polychrome, is usually ground with a quick-drying oil; otherwise, the result is apt to be tacky and to take a long time to dry. The unexpected and often interesting effects—

one might call them squashed effects—that ensue when the wet pigment is run through the press, provide the fascination of the medium and the challenge to control it. The seventeenth-century Italian artist Giovanni Castiglione seems to have been the first to make monotypes. Edgar Degas also explored the medium with distinguished success. An interesting variation of the process has been employed by Henri Matisse. Instead of painting the plate with pigment, he rolled it uniformly with black printer's ink and drew a linear design with a stylus or needle. The resulting monotype shows a white line drawing against the black. It sometimes happens that some of the brushed pigment still remains on the plate after the first printing and that a second impression of a monotype can be run off the press. This replica is but a ghost and pale reflection of the original conception, more or less in the nature of a *maculature*, which is a second sheet of paper run through a press to clean off the surplus ink from an intaglio plate after printing.

PLANOGRAPHIC PROCESS, or printing from a plane surface. See LITHOGRAPH.

PLASTER PRINT can refer either to an intaglio print made on plaster (plaster of Paris) instead of paper (see INTAGLIO PRINTING) or to a paper print made from a carved dental-plaster block. (See RELIEF PRINTING.)

RELIEF ETCHING. A name sometimes given to a print from a metal plate produced by etching away all but the design. The pages comprising Blake's Prophetic Books were made in this way. The artist painted his design and all the lettering (in reverse) on a copper plate with an acid-resisting varnish. The plate was put in an acid bath until enough of the exposed parts were etched away to bring the design in relief. The plate was printed as a woodcut.

RELIEF PRINTING (*impression en relief, Hochdruck*). The printing of woodcuts or wood engravings is accomplished by either of two methods. The simplest is by hand-rubbing or burnishing. The ink is applied to the surface of the block by a roller or brayer. A sheet of paper is laid on the face of the block, and the back of the paper is rubbed with a burnisher or even the back of a spoon, consistently in every direction, until the inked design is completely transferred to the paper. The ink is of the kind used in the printing of type and books, that is to say, somewhat less stiff than the ink used for intaglio printing. When a rather large edition of prints is required at one time, the block is printed in a press. Again, the press is of the kind used for printing type, such as a Washington hand press, any screw press, or even a cylinder proving press, but not a rotary press. Before the actual printing begins, some time must be devoted to what is called the "makeready." Since the pressure is vertical and uniform, and since the block may not be "true," the surface of the block must be made precisely parallel to the platen of the press; otherwise failures in contact and therefore in printing will occur. The makeready involves the pasting of sheets of paper of specific shapes to the underside of the block at the necessary spots to bring the block up to true. This usually requires repeated trials in proving. Once the block is aligned to produce a perfect proof, it is inked in the usual way, and the printing proceeds much more expeditiously by press than by hand. Various substances have been used to print from, such as wood, both natural and artificial (plywood), leather, linoleum, cardboard, metal, synthetic plastics, or dental plaster.

RELIEF PROCESSES. A general term that includes woodcuts, wood engravings, linoleum cuts, metal cuts, *manière criblée*, relief etchings, and also prints made from artificially created relief blocks, such as cardboard prints, and those cellocuts, epoxy prints, and collographs that employ the relief principle in printing. In a cardboard print, the design is created by gluing cardboard shapes on a plane surface; in collographs, various shapes of cardboard, textiles, string, and so on, are glued to the surface, and then covered with lacquer to be printed from. In cellocuts, epoxy prints, and the like, liquid celluloid, epoxy, acrylics, and other synthetic plastics are poured on a board or metal plate, and allowed to harden and set. The plastic reliefs thus created may be printed from, as in a woodcut, without manipulation, or they may be worked over with tools for further refinements. Some of the relief blocks can also be printed in the intaglio manner.

SERIGRAPHY (*sérigraphie*). A stencil process. The artist creates his stencil on a screen by the tusche wash-out method, for example. The screen consists of a piece of silk or synthetic textile stretched on a wooden frame and hinged to a wooden base. The artist draws his key design (or the first of his color separations) with lithographic tusche or crayon on the screen. Then the screen is thinly but completely covered with glue. When the glue has set, benzene (or kerosene) is poured on both the front and back of the sceen. The benzene dissolves and washes out the tusche drawing, but not the glue. An open-mesh stencil of the drawing is created. For printing, tempera or oil colors may be used. Prepared mediums, transparent base and reducing varnish, are used to thin the color; transparent base makes it print transparently, whereas reducing varnish makes it print opaquely.

A sheet of paper is laid on the wooden base under the screen, and a generous portion of pigment is laid along the edge of the screen (that has now been laid over the paper). A squeegee (a rubber blade with a wooden handle similar to a window cleaner) is run across the screen, forcing the pigment through the screen and onto the paper. When the required number have been printed, the paint is washed off the screen with benzene, and the glue with water, leaving the screen clean. The second stencil is drawn and printed.

The entire process is repeated until the whole color composition is built up. Serigraphy is specially adapted for color work, although Ben Shahn has used it effectively just with black lines. The characteristic mesh of the screen is visible when a print is examined with a magnifying glass, and is a distinguishing mark of the process. Serigraphy is part of the general method of silk-screen printing (which see), but the name serves to differentiate original artists' prints from commercial productions.

SILK-SCREEN PRINTING (*Siebdruck*). An improvement in the original stencil process was made around the beginning of the twentieth century: the master stencil was pasted on a stretched piece of silk. This made printing easier. The open mesh of the silk allowed the pigment to pass through without difficulty, and the silk, wherever attached to the stencil, gave firm support to the delicate strips and promontories that otherwise were easily torn. By this device one could anchor an island of opaque (like the middle of the figure *O*) in a sea of open mesh—which was impossible to do in a regular stencil. The essential characteristic of a cut stencil attached to a screen is sharpness of outline; silk-screen printing therefore has been much employed commercially for lettering and posters. Around 1939 Anthony Velonis and others on the Federal Art Project in New York adapted the process more specifically for artists' use, by dispensing with the cut stencil altogether and creating its equivalent by wash-out methods similar to lift-ground etching. For a description of the process, see SERIGRAPHY, above. People have been confused by the term silk-screen print, assuming that the prints are on silk. The word "silk" refers to the material of the screen, and not to the end product.

STENCIL (*pochoir, Schablone*). Stencils cut in paper or very thin sheets of metal, invented in China, were used to color popular prints in quantity in Europe from the fifteenth century on. From the old stencil process was developed the silk-screen printing method (which see). In France around the 1920's, however, an expert craftsman, J. Saudé, used the straight-stencil, or *pochoir*, process as a reproductive medium for illustrating books.

SOFT-GROUND ETCHING (*vernis mou, Weichgrundradierung, Durchdruckverfahren*). An intaglio process. A soft ground is prepared from hard ground by the addition of tallow or Vaseline to make it tacky and sticky in consistency. This ground, thinly applied to a copper plate, is now ready to receive impresses of various kinds. For instance, a sheet of paper is laid on the grounded plate and a drawing made on it with a pencil or stylus. The ground will adhere to the paper wherever a pencil mark has pressed down on it, and be lifted off with the paper, exposing the bare metal in a replica of the drawing, but with a characteristic crumbly line as translated through the texture of the paper. Impresses of many kinds of textiles, lace, wire, string, leaves, bark, wood grains, and other objects have also been made in soft ground. The plates are then bitten and printed in the usual way. The granular lines of soft-ground etching might be confused, under magnification, with those of a crayon lithograph, but they exhibit the very slight embossing characteristic of intaglio printing, and are unlike the surface effects produced by lithography. Both linear and textured or tonal effects can be created by soft ground.

STIPPLE PRINT (*estampe pointillé, Punktiermanier*) and other dotted processes. Stipple etching in its best known form was developed in England for reproductive purposes in the late eighteenth century. W. W. Ryland probably was the first, and Francesco Bartolozzi the most famous, practitioner. The design is built up by minute dots, through a grounded plate, produced either by hand with a needle or by a *roulette* or *moulette* with regular or irregular bite. The plate is then bitten in the usual way. Earlier in the century French reproductive engravers, such as Jean Charles François, Gilles Demarteau, and Louis-Marin Bonnet, produced similar prints, under the name of crayon manner, pastel or chalk manner, by the expert use of such tools as the *grattoir* (mace-head), *roulette* (spur wheel), and *moulette* (drum roulette), supplemented by needles and burins. Stipple engraving, or more correctly flick engraving, is performed on an ungrounded plate, generally with a special tool called a stippling burin (with a curved shank). Some of Giulio Campagnola's prints of the early sixteenth century display tiny flicks or short jabs into the copper. Dots and flicks were also used by Ottavio Leoni, Robert Nanteuil, and other portrait engravers.

SUGAR-LIFT ETCHING. See LIFT-GROUND ETCHING.

WOODCUT (*gravure sur bois, taille d'épargne, Holzschnitt*). The earliest of the relief processes. The earliest dated woodcut extant in the East is dated 868, in the West, the so-called *Brussels Madonna* of 1418. In the past, the designer made his drawing with a quill pen directly on the wood or the drawing on paper was pasted on the block, whereupon another craftsman, called a *Formschneider*, cut away, down to a depth of one eighth of an inch, all of the surface except the design itself. Today the original artist both designs and cuts his own block. Various kinds of wood were used, such as pear, apple, sycamore, or beech. The block was cut plankwise (*bois de fil, Langholz*), that is, along the length of the grain or tree trunk. A knife (*canif, Messer*) is the chief tool used. Four strokes are necessary to define a line on the block. The cut is at an angle away from the line on either side; the incisions are disengaged and turned into a shaving by another oblique cut on each side. Large areas are cleared with chisels and gouges. Lines can be cut with a V-shaped chisel, thus performing two operations of the knife in one stroke, but care must be taken not to work against the grain for fear of splintering the wood. The printing of a block is described under RELIEF PRINTING.

WOOD ENGRAVING (*gravure sur bois debout, Hirnholzstich, Holzstich*). A variant of woodcut. In the cutting of a plank-wise block, one is apt to encounter difficulties with the grain: A knife stroke against the grain is sometimes deflected or causes splintering, and requires great skill and strength to control. To overcome this, printmakers in England around the beginning of the eighteenth century began to prepare their blocks in a different way: They utilized the cross section of the tree trunk and worked on the end grain (*bois debout, Hirnholz*). The grain, now running up and down the thickness of the block, offers no resistance to cutting in any direction. Since harder woods, such as boxwood or maple, can be used, and since engraving tools, instead of the knife, can be employed, much finer detail and texture can be achieved. Prints from such blocks are called wood engravings.

A woodcut, in general, is linear and strong in contrasts of black and white. With wood engraving one can obtain a greater range of color values, as it were: many semitints or shades of gray, as well as black and white. A white line against black can be obtained with one stroke of the engraver's burin or its modifications, the spitsticker and tint tool. The Englishman Thomas Bewick was not the first to employ the technique, but he used it so consistently and established its practice so firmly that his name is generally associated with wood engraving as opposed to woodcutting. In the nineteenth century wood engraving was much used as a reproductive medium in connection with book illustration. Some artists, however, have made original wood engravings, notably Gauguin, and recently Rockwell Kent, Leonard Baskin, and Misch Kohn. The difference between woodcut and wood engraving is not always clear. Some hold that the difference lies in the artist's basic conception of his picture: In a woodcut he works in terms of black lines or areas against a background of white; in a wood engraving, in terms of white lines against a background of black. It sometimes happens that the artist uses both methods in the same picture, and then it becomes difficult to say which predominates. The other school holds that the difference lies in the technique. Woodcuts are printed from plankwise blocks cut with a knife, whereas wood engravings are printed from end-grain blocks cut with a burin. This classification at least has the virtue of not being ambiguous: the artist cannot combine end-grain and along-the-grain on the same block. Though it is not always easy to tell what kind of wood was used just by looking at a print, one can usually tell whether the artist used a knife or burin. The printing is described under RELIEF PRINTING.

2. OTHER TERMS RELATING TO PRINTS

Note: These notes refer mostly to old prints, and are included chiefly to enlighten the general collector.

ABBREVIATIONS. A few terms found on prints, chiefly of the past, and in Latin:

del., delineavit: has drawn it
exc., *excud.*, excudit: has published it
fec., *f.*, fecit: has made it (usually engraved)
formis, in the stock of the publisher
H. C., hors commerce: not for sale
imp., impressit: has printed it (on modern prints, usually written in pencil)
inc., incisit: has engraved it
inv., invenit: has designed it
lith., drew or printed on stone, an ambiguous reference, not differentiating between draftsman and printer

pinx., pinxit: has painted it
sculp., *sc.*, sculpsit: has engraved it

ARTIST'S PROOFS. See under Chapter V, "The Artist and the Print Market."

CATALOGUE REFERENCES. A considerable portion of old master prints have been catalogued and exactly described in various general catalogues and lexicons. The most famous of these is Adam Bartsch's monumental work *Le Peintre-graveur* in twenty-one volumes, Vienna 1803–1821. It is still in use today, and a specific print, let us say, Dürer's engraving *Melancolia,* is located and referred to as Bartsch No. 74. Of course, not all extant prints appear in his *catalogue raisonné,* and many other general works have appeared as a continuation of his pioneer compilation, not to mention innumerable monographs on the works of individual artists. Thus the print lover will find references, in sale catalogues or museum exhibitions, to such names as J. K. Nagler, J. D. Passavant, Charles Le Blanc, Max Lehrs, A. M. Hind, A. P. F. Robert-Dumesnil (*Peintre-graveur français*), A. de Vesme (*Peintre-graveur italien*), A. von Wurzbach (Dutch), Henri Beraldi (nineteenth century), or Loys Delteil (nineteenth and twentieth centuries). In a *catalogue raisonné* one may expect to find a description of the print, a reproduction of it (in more recent works), and other information regarding date, dimensions, technique, states, sometimes the size of the edition, and enumeration of copies.

COLLECTOR'S MARKS. Collectors of the past and present have often affixed a mark or monogram on their prints. They are usually placed on the back of the print, but occasionally appear on the front—which, alas, detracts from the aesthetic effect of the print. Such marks add considerable associative interest to a print, since they provide a clue to its provenance or past history, and even to its authenticity. A print that once belonged to a famous connoisseur or collector is thus endowed with an additional cachet of quality. Most museum collections also have their marks; and occasionally prints bearing such marks appear on the market, when the museum in question disposed of a duplicate from its collection. Sometimes it is possible to trace, through its collector's mark, a print that has been stolen from a museum. All these marks have been gathered together and catalogued in a monumental work by Frits Lugt entitled *Les Marques de Collections*, Amsterdam, 1921. This book and the later supplementary volume are a mine of information regarding the history of collecting, the scope of museum holdings, and the mutations of taste. The proud but inexperienced collector, intending to put his mark on his prints, is warned not to use the ordinary, commercially available stamping pad as his source of ink, since such pads contain not ink but a dye that has great penetrating power and may show up on the face of the print to its disfigurement. The only ink to use is printing ink, and if the paper is fairly transparent, care should be taken to place it on a spot where it will not show through.

COLORING BY HAND. Some of the oldest known prints were colored by hand, and the practice has continued off and on until today. For instance, flower prints of the seventeenth and eighteenth centuries were often colored by hand, and so were the earlier Currier and Ives prints, before they were produced by chromolithography. Likewise, some of William Blake's works exist that are hand colored, either by him or by his wife. There is nothing reprehensible about coloring by hand; in fact, it often enhances the beauty of the prints. But the question of hand coloring as against printing in color does raise some problems of connoisseurship. When a print is published, printed in color, there can be little doubt that the colors represent the artist's intention and choice. If, however, the print is represented as colored by the artist himself, how is one to know, except by explicit proof? The difference between a print colored by Blake and one by his wife should be considerable in terms of aesthetic merit and monetary value, yet the only verification generally offered is by attribution.

Where a great artist's handiwork is not involved, such as in a flower print or a view, the problem hinges upon whether the coloring is old and contemporary with the making of the print, or whether it is recent—again a difference in value. Prints, either late restrikes from the plate or genuine old uncolored impressions, have often been colored by a later hand. Only an eye trained by study and long experience can discriminate between coloring that is authentic or "true" and that which is modern.

FACSIMILES OF RARE PRINTS. See under PROCESS PRINTS, *Hand Photogravure*.

HELIOGRAPH. See under PROCESS PRINTS, *Hand Photogravure*.

NUMBERING PRINTS. The conventional notation is generally written thus (7/35) meaning the seventh of an edition of thirty-five. For a general discussion of the problem of numbering, see Chapter V, "The Artist and the Print Market."

ORIGINAL PRINT. An original print is one that the artist has executed after his own invention. The artist performs every step in the creation of a master design on an appropriate medium from which impressions can be taken. The medium may be a metal plate, stone slab, wood block, or other material suitable for making multi-original works of art. The impressions or prints are made from the master design by the artist himself or pursuant to his directions. The print should be signed in pencil by the artist as a guarantee that it is an original print by him. See further discussion in Chapter V, "The Artist and the Print Market."

PAPER. Paper is an important ingredient in printmaking.

Without it, the art would never have developed to the extent it has, for it provides a durable, cheap, and universally available vehicle for the printing of pictures and all letterpress. Other materials have been used—parchment or vellum, namely, the prepared skin of animals, and silk and linen—but they are either expensive or not especially suitable for the purpose. The technical handbooks on printmaking describe the papers best adapted for the various mediums in use today. But a few general notes on the types of paper and their history may be useful to collectors. The literature on papermaking is extensive, and the interested reader is referred to the bibliographies in Dard Hunter's *Papermaking* (New York, Knopf, 1947), which also has served as a source for much of the information outlined below. Papermaking was invented in China around the beginning of the second century of the Christian Era, but the secret of its manufacture did not reach Europe until the middle of the twelfth century under the Saracens in Spain. By the beginning of the fifteenth century, paper mills were in operation in Italy, France, Germany, and the Netherlands.

Paper, in general, is a thin sheet of cellulose fibers thoroughly mixed and tangled together as in a felting operation. Cellulose comes from the woody parts of plants, in other words, the cell walls, freed from all foreign substances. There are many sources for fibers: raw materials, such as the bark of the paper mulberry tree, bamboo, flax, hemp, jute, cotton, various straws (rice, for instance), esparto grass, wood pulp (only in the last hundred years); and partially processed materials, such as linen (flax), silk, and cotton rags. The fibers must be freed from the glutinous, resinous, and other intercellular impurities by beating, pounding, macerating, cooking with wood ashes and, in Occidental practice, with chemical bleaches. Rags, already partly processed, are treated with an alkaline solution to remove traces of grease due to human contact, but do not

[63]

require so much drastic treatment to disintegrate the fibers. The purified fibers suspended in water are placed in a vat.

The basic operations of making paper may then be summarized as follows: The essential tool is the papermaking mold, consisting of a wooden frame, within which a system of crisscross wires is stretched: *chain* lines running up and down the short dimensions of the sheet and spaced from one half to two inches apart, and *laid* lines running the long way, and spaced from about twenty to forty to the inch. There is also the *deckle*, a removable wooden frame or fence around the edge of the mold, which keeps the fibers in, and determines the size of the sheet of paper and its deckle edge. The *vatman* dips the mold, with deckle attached, in the vat and brings it up horizontally, filled with fiber to the desired thickness, and running over with water. After an operation known as the *shake*, a lateral motion from right to left, and forward, from back to front, designed further to intertwine and felt the fibers, he removes the deckle and hands the frame, still dripping, to the *coucher*, who continues the draining process, and by a skillful maneuver flicks the wet sheet from the mold to a thick felt drying pad, slightly larger than the sheet. The felt of the pad has no causal relation to the felting operation of the fibers in the paper; the pad is merely the vehicle for handling and drying.

The vatman meanwhile has continued his dipping operation for the next sheet. When 144 sheets have been formed, they and their protective pads (the stack being known as the *post*) are conveyed to a press to squeeze out more water. After undergoing a series of drying, sizing, and surfacing operations, they emerge as sheets of handmade paper (*papier à la cuve* [vat], *Büttenpapier* [*Butte*, vat], *geschöpftes Papier*). The coating of *size* consists of a thin application of gelatin or glue, in order to render the paper more opaque or impervious. Otherwise, the paper would be highly absorbent, or similar to blotting or filter paper. Most Chinese and Japanese papers (except the so-called *Japanese vellum* or *Imperial Japan*) are unsized or slightly sized—a condition that suits their requirements, for their writing tool is the brush and their medium for type and illustration is the woodcut. Most Oriental books are printed on one side of the sheet only, and then folded over, the fold appearing on the outside edge of the book. In the culture of the Western world, as Dard Hunter has pointed out, the writing tool is the pen, and the bookmaking method is letterpress from metal type, printed on both sides of the sheet, thus calling for a full-bodied opaque paper.

The type of handmade paper described above is known as *laid* paper (*papier vergé, Büttenpapier?*) in contradistinction to *wove* paper (*velin, Velinpapier*). Both types refer to the construction of the mold and its screen, and not to any operation in the actual manufacture of the paper. (Some people have thoughtlessly assumed that paper could be woven.) The earliest form of screen used by the Chinese probably was a stretched piece of coarsely woven cloth, with its characteristic regular pattern of warp and woof, thus producing a wove paper. Later, laid screens made of thin slivers of bamboo bound together with horsehair were employed. This speeded the process of manufacture, since the wet fibers suspended on a textile screen could not be quickly *couched*, but had to remain on the screen for a much longer period until almost completely dry. As paper manufacture developed in Europe, metal wires were substituted for the bamboo-horsehair combinations, but its formal pattern was retained. Therefore all early paper in Europe was of the *laid* variety. The mark of the screen is visible, when a sheet is held up against the light, in the form of slightly more translucent lines, known as wire lines or laid lines. The impress arises because the paper is slightly thinner wherever the wires project. By the same principle a watermark (*filigrane, Wasserzeichen*)—namely, a

[65]

monogram or other device made of wire and laced to the screen—can be incorporated in the paper. Watermarks in general were inserted to indicate the manufactory, and have sometimes been useful in determining the date and place of origin. The earliest Oriental papers had no watermark, but in recent times Japanese papers do.

A kind of natural paper, not fabricated by human hands, occurs in nature. The nest, or housing, of the papermaking wasp is made of a substance having all the characteristics of paper. In 1719, the French scientist Ferchault de Réamur called attention to the ability of wasps to make paper from trees, and suggested wood pulp as a possible source for paper. The problem was in the air, for the supply of linen and cotton rags, hitherto the only available source, was becoming scarcer and scarcer, owing to the increasing demand for paper. Other substances, such as jute, various grasses and straws, were tried and used in limited quantities; but methods for tapping the enormous potential source in wood pulp were not perfected until the middle of the nineteenth century. The disadvantage of wood pulp lay in the difficulty of eliminating *lignin*, the resinous intercellular tissue of wood. The production of a reasonably white paper involved the use of strong chemical bleaches, the sulfites, in other words, sulfurous acid. It was found impossible to remove all traces of the chemicals, which consequently remained, and in time stained whatever they came in contact with. Wood pulp, also, was not durable, and tended to become brittle and crumbly with age. But it was cheap and the supply unlimited. It is the newsprint of our day. Wood-pulp papers are of little concern to print collectors except in so far as they are dangerous in contact with fine prints. Cheap cardboard mats of sulfite papers, especially when the print is mounted down solidly on them, will eventually discolor and otherwise damage the print. The use of mounts made of all-rag paper, although expensive, will obviate this difficulty.

Another step that revolutionized the papermaking industry was the invention of machine-made paper. Beginning with Nicolas Louis Robert's patent of 1798, machinery was perfected that eventually compressed all the operations of papermaking into one continuous and speedy process, including the laying and the felting of the fibers (*shaking*), drying by suction and heat, sizing (added to the pulp), surfacing of the paper by calender rolls, and even the imprint of watermarks (by means of a *dandy roll*). Most paper today is machine made, and of the *wove* type, because the endless belt of the machine mold is made of a woven wire screen. The wire lines in wove paper when the sheet is held up to the light are very often impossible to distinguish, especially when the paper has been calendered. In the absence of distinctive *laid* marks, one may assume that the paper is wove. The manufacture of handmade wove paper was introduced into Europe around the middle of the eighteenth century by the English papermaker J. Whatman, probably at the instigation of the printer John Baskerville. Most of the fine prints of the past and present are on handmade paper of the best quality, either laid or wove, since the artists are among the few people who prefer to work with the more expensive but purer varieties of paper.

In printmaking, European papers are more often employed than Oriental. But Japanese paper is well adapted for modern woodcuts and even etchings (some of Rembrandt's finest proofs were on Japan). Chinese papers have also been used for printing woodcuts and lithographs. Oriental papers come in various weights from heavy to thin. The thin varieties have a limited use in printmaking (though not in bookmaking) unless they are backed up by a heavier piece of paper, in the form known in English as India laid. At the time it was introduced, the English were in the habit of calling anything from the Orient as Indian (India ink, for example). The thin India paper is really from China. The French were more accurate: They called the paper *chine collée*. One further note about a so-called Chinese rice paper, which is not a paper at all and could not be used for printmaking: Also called Formosa paper, it was imported by the tea merchants and clipper ships from China in the early nineteenth century. On these fragile sheets are usually depicted genre scenes, the trades of China and the like, in the brilliant colors of the realistic Canton school. The sheeets, exceedingly brittle and seldom now found intact, actually are not paper at all, but the inner pith of a tree, *Fatsia papyfera*.

PHOTOGRAPHY. Although photomechanical methods of reproduction have been discussed in this booklet, nothing has been said about photography itself as a form of printmaking. For photography is a form of printmaking, and, like the other print mediums, is capable of both utilitarian and aesthetic use. In the early nineteenth century the researches of Louis Daguerre, Nicéphore Niepce, William Talbot, and others brought about the perfection of the photographic process—a device for fixing an image on paper or glass plate, and later on film, by purely optical and chemical means, and then printing from that negative. The *daguerreotype*, being a unique positive, cannot be classed as a print. The camera can objectively and impersonally translate whatever appears before it in terms of light and dark upon the plate. The subjective factor is the selective eye of the photographer. If nature, or any object, is to be copied, photography can do it more quickly and cheaply than any artist can. And seemingly more accurately, because the copyist's personality is not obvious. It must be remembered, however, that photography is really only another pictorial convention and that the camera's eye also has a kind of "personality" or idiosyncrasy, since its diverse-angled lenses and monocular vision (as opposed to human binocular or stereoscopic vision) produce not only variations but also distortion from "reality." But photography is so universally used and accepted that we have adopted its conventions as the last word in accuracy or "realism."

Today, photography is the great documentary medium. Although most of its applications have been utilitarian and documentary, the medium has been employed to create original and conscious works of art, in other words, original prints. Witness the prints of such master photographers as Alfred Stieglitz or Edward Weston, to name but two. It has been said that photography could not be an art medium because all its operations are mechanical. All the print mediums have mechanical elements, which the artist has learned to manipulate and control. There are enough variations in the steps of the photographic process to give the artist a wide repertory of expressive devices: lighting and arrangement of materials, choice of lenses, changes of focus, variations in development and printing, including solarization. There is no logical reason, then, why a photograph cannot be a work of art if it is made by a conscious artist. The subject is vast and complex and could easily fill a book. It is introduced here briefly for the sake of completeness.

PRINTING QUALITY. There can be good or bad impressions of a print, and the eyes of a connoisseur can discriminate between them. The problem is more pertinent to old master prints than to contemporary production, since the modern artist publishes relatively few prints in his edition, and each of them is usually well printed. Except for careless and slipshod operations, most inferior printing is due to the deterioration of the plate or block.

The thin lines in relief on a wood block, for instance, can break down under prolonged pressure and destroy the readability of the design. Wood blocks warp or are attacked by worms. One sometimes sees old woodcuts by Dürer—old, but printed much later than Dürer's time—where the blank wormholes are clearly visible. All such impressions are inferior. Large flat areas of tone in a woodcut are probably the most difficult to print. It is desirable, for instance, to achieve a rich, vibrant black—not a uniform dead black, but one with minute variations, as if alive. In all mediums a good quality of paper is essential.

Continued wiping of a copperplate, as well as the pressure of the press, wears down the metal, rendering the etched or engraved lines shallower, and making the inked lines in them thinner and weaker. The minute projecting ridges of metal on a drypoint plate are especially vulnerable. The difference, for example, between an etching printed in Rembrandt's studio and the same subject printed a hundred or so years later is startling. One is but a ghost, a travesty upon the original, especially when the plate has been reworked by another hand to restore the lines to a normal depth. The beauty of an etched proof is dependent upon an exquisite harmony between the color and texture of the paper and the color and consistency of the ink, upon the delicate balance between inking and wiping, and upon the adjusted pressure of the press. Insufficient ink in the lines and irrelevant smudges on the plate are generally signs of careless printing. Color printing presents special problems of registry in all the mediums. Wherever the superposition of the successive color plates is not perfect, the printing must be accounted inferior.

Prolonged inking and rolling of a lithograph stone is apt to cause the locked-in grease to spread, thereby clogging and coarsening the minute dots that make up the design. If the stone is re-etched to fix the grease again, the acid is apt to eat up some of the more delicate particles, and bring about losses in the design. A comparison between a proof before letters of a Daumier lithograph and an impression from *Chari-vari* on inferior paper will show how great a loss is possible.

It must be kept in mind, however, that a print, even if not

of the finest quality of printing, is nevertheless still an original print. A lithograph by Daumier from the magazine *Charivari* or an etching by Piranese from the *Calcografia*, even though it is printed in quantity and not well printed, is still technically an original print.

The feeling for printing quality comes only by long experience, deliberate study, and repeated comparisons between various impressions of the same subject. The discrimination between good and bad printing can be a fascinating pastime.

PROCESS PRINTS. All prints made by photomechanical methods are called process prints. By definition, they are not original prints, but since they have some similarities, in duplicating principle or printing method, with original prints, and are sometimes confused with them, it would seem advisable to describe them briefly. No attempt will be made to describe the techniques in detail, since they are either trade secrets or are explicitly treated in professional manuals. The following notes are partly based on Harold Curwen's *Processes of Graphic Reproduction in Printing*:

Line Block—(*chemitypie, cliché trait, Strichätzung, Strichcliché*). The line block is the simplest of the photoreproductive processes. It can be used to reproduce only pictures with strong contrasts of black and white (no semitints), and thus bears a close analogy with the woodcut medium. A polished zinc plate is coated with an emulsion of albumin or gelatin, mixed with potassium bichromate. The emulsion hardens on exposure to light. A photographic negative of the subject to be reproduced is then placed in contact with the sensitized plate, and exposed to light. The light, passing unrestricted through the transparent parts of the negative (corresponding to the dark lines and areas of the original image) will harden the albumin emulsion, whereas those areas of the emulsion that are

[71]

protected from the light by the dense black of the negative will remain in their original soluble state. The zinc is then rolled over with a greasy ink and soaked in water. The albumin, which has not been hardened by the action of light, dissolves away, carrying the ink with it. The plate is dried and dusted with powdered rosin, which adheres to the ink left on the image. The rosin is melted or baked on the plate to form an acid resist. The plate is etched several times in an acid bath until the background has been eaten away to a depth sufficient to prevent it from touching the paper in the printing machine. In other words, the equivalent of a wood block has been produced photographically on a metal plate. An early variant of the line block was perfected around the middle of the nineteenth century in France by Claude Gillot, and hence called *gillotype*. The image was produced on the zinc plate by mechanical transfer methods rather than by photography. Some of the later Daumier lithographs were transferred to *gillotype* and appeared in *Charivari* as a cheaper shortcut in printing, since such reproductions could be printed in the same *forme* as the letterpress.

Halftone Block—(*autotypie, cliché-simili en relief, Rasterdruck, Netzätzung*). This technique bears some resemblance to nineteenth-century, white-line reproductive wood engraving. It is a method for "splitting the continuous tone of the original into a mass of tiny individual dots of varying size, which, when printed, produce the optical impression of a graduated tone of smooth texture." The key operation is the interposition of a screen (*trame, Raster*) between the camera and the object to be reproduced. The screen, of glass, has a series of fine lines regularly laid at right angles. This device creates an enormous (up to about 25,000 per square inch) number of small windows of clear glass, through which the image comes to the plate, broken up into dots of varying size. The resulting negative is printed on a sensitized copperplate, and the other steps of wash-out and etch applied, as described under Line Block. But the metal plate is of copper and not of zinc. Screens can be coarse (50 lines per inch) or fine (up to 175 lines per inch), according to the size of the "windows," ranging from newsprint pictures, where the screen is obvious, to fine work on coated paper where it can hardly be distinguished with the naked eye. The regular pattern of the screen is a distinguishing mark in halftone blocks, rotogravure, some photogravure, most photolithography, but not in line blocks, collotypes, and certain hand photogravures. The finer-screened varieties of halftone plates must be printed on coated paper for the best effect. The paper has been loaded or coated with kaolin, clay, or other substances, and highly calendered.

Rotogravure—(héliogravure rotative, Rakeltiefdruck Schnellpressen photogravur). In the rotogravure process the plate is in the form of a copperplated cylinder, functioning in a web-fed rotary press for long and speedy runs of printing. A reversed halftone screen is used, with a grid of transparent lines but opaque black squares. On exposure to light, the emulsion on the copperplate hardens under the lines, but the squares remain soft. Exposed again under a diapositive (not a negative but a photographic positive transparency of the subject), the squares harden in proportion to the range of grays. After etching, the dots appear as squares of equal size but varying depth, and will hold varying amounts of thin volatile ink to create the gradations of tone in the print. The pattern of the screen on the copperplated cylinder is thus raised in crossed lines that serve as a bearing surface for the scraping blade or *doctor* (*raclette*, *Rakel*) which removes the ink from the surface following the rotation of the cylinder in a trough of ink. The grid of fine crossed lines is therefore light in tone, and is visible under magnification. This is the mark by which rotogravure may be recognized. The volatile ink dries partly by absorption but mainly by quick evaporation. It is therefore largely on the surface of the paper, and does not appear minutely raised above the paper in the way intaglio prints do.

Hand Photogravure or *Heliograph*—(*héliogravure*, *Heliogravur*). An earlier and less mechanical process that does not use a halftone screen. Powdered rosin or bitumen is dusted over and melted on the copperplate, very much as in aquatint. A bichromate-gelatin emulsion is laid over the grounded plate and exposed to light through a halftone diapositive. The other operations proceed in more or less the usual way. Because a diapositive, instead of a negative, is used, the tonal scale is reversed; the lightest portions of the original will act on the emulsion to produce the maximum hardness and consequently the greatest resistance to the action of the mordant. The least exposed parts (darkest in the original) cannot be eaten away in broad flat masses of dark because of the bitumen granulation, which ensures the keeping of a grained surface even in the darkest passages. The wiping of ink is done by hand, as is the printing in a hand press. The process can yield very fine and quite faithful facsimiles, including reproductions of old master etchings. This was the method employed in producing the facsimiles of rare old prints by Amand-Durand, the *Reichsdruckerei*, and the like. They were made for study and not as counterfeits, because they usually have a distinguishing mark on the back of the print. But mounted down solidly on cardboard and framed under glass, they have sometimes passed as originals, either in ignorance or by fraudulent intent. But the paper is modern, and the "feel," in general, is not that of an original. The lines are slightly raised as in intaglios, but, when examined with a glass, lack depth and subtlety of bite. An engraved line loses its character, since it is produced by etching and not by the burin. Woodcuts suffer less by reproduction and are therefore more deceptive, but the paper is always the telltale mark.

Collotype—(phototypie, artotypie, Lichtdruck, Glasdruck, Albertotypie.) The process bears some resemblance to lithography. The lines of collotype in the reproduction of a print have the characteristics of surface printing: They are flat and lack depth. But no screen is required for collotype, and it can be printed on any kind of paper. The distinguishing feature of the process is that the glass plate with two coatings (one of them the usual gelatin-bichromate emulsion) becomes the actual printing surface. The image of the original is printed on the plate through a diapositive transparency, as usual, but there is no subsequent washout. The plate is so constituted that certain areas—to the extent and degree that the bichromate emulsion is not hardened by exposure to light—absorbs moisture. Ink, rolled over the finished plate, will stick on the hardened parts (and all the degrees of semihardness) and be rejected on all the moistened parts by the same principle that applies to lithography. The process requires expert manipulation and rigid control of temperature and atmospheric moisture, but it reproduces with considerable fidelity all the gradations of tone in the original.

Photolithographic Offset. An application of lithographic techniques to commercial and quantity production. An image can be photographed onto a stone, or better yet to a zinc plate, by the interpolation of a screen. The resulting reproduction can be printed in the usual way by hand inking and hand printing. Manual printing takes time, and the process can be expedited by recourse to an offset printing machine. This is a rotary press, and consequently only zinc or aluminum plates can be used, capable of being bent around a cylinder. The offset principle is a double printing. The inked image from the zinc plate is printed on a rubber blanket or roller, which in turn prints it on a sheet or roll of paper. The ink used is rather thin to facilitate quick inking and easy transfer. Sharp hairlines come through with little loss, but dark areas of tone are apt to be somewhat "grayed." The image, twice reversed, appears as in the zinc plate.

PROOF BEFORE LETTERS (*avant la lettre, vor der Schrift*). In the past, many reproductive prints were issued with certain indications engraved in the lower margins. Such information might consist of the name of the engraver, the name of the artist after whose painting the engraving was made, the name and address of the publisher of the print, and an elaborate dedication to a patron. The lettering was usually done last, and the plate sent to a professional letter engraver. The prints before letters, especially with mezzotints before the invention of steel-facing, would be earlier and therefore better in printing quality. Publishers were not unaware of the commercial possibilities, and a regular series of steps were evolved: proofs before all letters, scratched letter proofs, open letter proofs, proofs before the address or dedication, ending up with the ordinary lettered impressions. There have also been instances where some enterprising person obtained an old plate, polished off all the lettering, and issued so-called proofs before all letters. The worn state of the plate usually belied the representation.

RARITY. A comparative term, sometimes misused, especially in its superlative degree: unique. The late dealer and expert Harry Bland used to say, "So you have a unique print; well, I have one that's uniquer." It must be remembered that rarity is measured by known and extant examples, and there is always a likelihood that another may turn up. The odds, however, against such a possibility are becoming longer and longer, as time goes on. Indeed, it is a miracle that so many prints have survived the hazards of neglect, fire, war, and other catastrophes. A striking instance of this is shown in the example of a woodcut certificate of membership in a benevolent association known as the Confrérie Royale de la Charité de Notre Dame de Bonne Déliverance. Jean Michel Papillon, in his *Histoire de la Gravure en Bois* of 1766, cites this woodcut as an example of a block so well engraved by him that it had at the date of writing yielded over five hundred thousand impressions. Another source, Abbé Gaston in his book *Images de Confréries Parisiennes*, points out that of the multitude printed, only three impressions are known to exist today. No one disputes that all old prints are rare and that some are rarer than others, but it does not follow that scarcity is the sole criterion of worth, as in postage stamps. Rarity is a factor, but only one factor, in estimating the value of a print. Of much greater significance are aesthetic or historic importance, attractiveness, beauty, or whatever it is that makes us like a print. A collector should not buy a print just because it is rare. One is reminded of a saying by a wise old dealer, Frederick Keppel, "There are some prints that are rare because not well done."

RESTORATION OF PRINTS. The problem comes up in two ways, the first of which is the need, chiefly in connection with old prints. The cleaning and restoration of dirty and damaged works is a task requiring much knowledge, training, and experience. The amateur is well advised to take the problem to a professional. The care of prints, their matting and framing, is a large subject in itself, and is properly discussed elsewhere, in Chapter VII. There is, however, one admonition that cannot be repeated too often. Do not, under any circumstances, ever use Scotch Tape on the front or back of prints. It is an inefficient adhesive, and leaves a permanent and damaging stain on whatever it touches.

The collector is more apt to encounter restorations already accomplished, in an occasional print offered for sale. The blemishes most often found are tears and thin spots mended, holes restored, spots of ink or oil removed, margins repaired or altered. It is wise to look at the back of a print or through it, before purchasing an old print. Not that there is anything wrong about a restored print; it is merely that one should know what one is getting. Many of the great paintings of the past, the Mona Lisa, for example, have come down to us in a restored state. We have even grown to love our Greek statues without arms or legs. If the restoration is well done—and it generally is—it will not necessarily detract from the aesthetic appeal of the print. It should, however, detract from the monetary value; and this fact is usually reflected in the price asked, which should be less than that of a comparable print in perfect condition. In this way a collector with a slender purse can sometimes acquire a rare print of otherwise good quality—a bargain not possible with a perfect print.

RESTRIKE. A print from an old plate, block, or stone made after, and generally long after, the original edition was issued. Restrikes are generally inferior, but are fraudulent only if sold as early printings. It is a reason why plates or blocks should be destroyed after the edition has been printed. The identification of restrikes requires an experienced eye, the chief factors being the quality of the printing and the age of the paper.

REVERSAL OF IMAGE. In the printing operation the image that the artist drew on the stone, block, or plate is reversed on the print. It becomes a mirror image: The right hand, for instance, becomes the left hand, and lettering is backward. In many cases it makes little difference in which sense the print is viewed, but in some cases it does. When an artist draws a street scene directly on an etching plate, all the familiar landmarks are jumbled. There is a way to overcome the reversal of image. The artist can copy his sketch in a mirror, or he can draw the same street scene with lithographic crayon on transfer paper—in which case, he can transfer the drawing onto a lithographic stone—a reversal of image—and then from the stone to the lithographic print—another reversal, making two, and bringing the image back to its original sense. If an artist wishes to put his name in the body of his composition, he must reverse it on the actual plate; artists sometimes forget, and the name appears backward. To summarize: In all relief and intaglio prints, the image is reversed, as well as in lithographs drawn directly upon the stone. The image is not reversed in a serigraph, or in a lithograph that began as a drawing transferred to stone, or was printed by offset.

STATES. An artist, while working on a plate or stone, may have occasion to check on what he is doing and print an impression from the unfinished plate. If he prints a sequence of trial proofs, they constitute the "states," or stages, through which the plate has passed. In some cases he may draw or sketch on these trials to test what he wants to do next. At any rate, they are usually few in number, since they are working proofs. He may or may not preserve them—some artists do not —but if they are preserved and eventually appear on the market, these rare states do give some insight into the artist's way of working. They have also appealed to collectors, for they are undoubtedly early proofs and rare, and have an intimate personal connection with the artist. But they may or may not be aesthetically satisfying, since, after all, the artist will not have realized his complete intention until the final version. Many artists of the past have worked their way through various states, adding a few lines here, eliminating a passage there, without being very self-conscious about marking them as states. But their whole work (at least, all available impressions) has been carefully studied and a sequence of states established *ex post facto*. For instance, elaborately illustrated catalogues have been published of the work of Rembrandt and Whistler, whose habit of work produced a revealing profusion of states.

The study of states has been useful in another important way, namely, in determining the sequence of printings. The plates of many of the old masters were never canceled, but were printed from, long after their deaths. As the plates wore down, they were often reworked by other hands to restore their usefulness, or other indications were added, such as the name of the publisher who bought them to add to his stock, or *fond*, of plates to be printed from. Therefore, a proper sequence of states can provide us with some information as to whether a certain print was produced during the artist's lifetime. There is a little confusion as to the difference between a trial proof and a state. Trial proofs are those prints made before the completion of the finished picture, and are therefore a subordinate part of the general term "state," which includes any change in the plate, whether by deliberate intent or by deterioration, during its entire existence. In modern times, when the cancellation of a plate after printing is common practice, there can be trial proofs in several states, but no states that are not trial proofs. In enumerating states, a convention with Roman numerals in lower case is sometimes employed. Thus, i/iii means the first state of three.

STEEL ENGRAVING. Engraving on steel plates is discussed here, rather than among the techniques of printmaking, because it is no longer in use as a medium. Engravings in general are often mistakenly referred to as steel engravings, when as a matter of fact the use of steel was strictly limited in point of time. The practice of reproductive engraving on steel arose in the early nineteenth century from the demand for a larger number of prints than could be obtained from a copperplate without wear. Steel is of course much tougher and harder to work upon, and mechanical aids, such as ruling machines, were often resorted to. Steel engravings are apt to be gray and cold, and very mannered in their engraving technique. After the invention of steel-facing, around 1857, there was no need to use steel, since the electrolytic coating of hard iron over a copperplate could give it the strength and durability of steel.

STONE RUBBING (also stone print and brass rubbing). A process that bears some resemblance to relief printing and that might possibly have been the forerunner of true relief or woodcut printing in China. Rubbings have been mainly reproductive in purpose, but are mentioned here on the chance that some artist may have used or will use the medium in a creative way. The distinctive feature consists of applying the ink to the back of the print instead of its face next to the block. It was first used to make copies of the texts of Confucian classics, engraved on stone tablets. Later, designs by Chinese artists were also reproduced. In the West, rubbings from old English memorial brasses and from old New England tombstones exist.

Damp paper is laid on the stone (or wood block) into which the design has been incised. The pliable paper is partially forced into the hollows with a stiff brush. Black ink (or color) is then rolled or dabbed over the exposed face of the paper (not the side next to the stone). The print is lifted off and dried. The incised lines appear white against a dark background—a kind of white-line woodcut. The image is not reversed as it would be if the color were applied directly to the block.

V

The Artist and the Print Market

THE NEED FOR STANDARD PROCEDURES

THE PRINT COUNCIL is concerned with eradicating certain dubious practices that have arisen in the commerce of prints, and appeals to the artists to help the Council in its crusade. The establishment of a fair and workable code of standards will benefit the artist in the long run, if it is scrupulously observed. A sound and uniform procedure will inspire confidence in the buyer—a matter in which the artist has a definite stake. The artist is primarily concerned with the creation of works of art, and only secondarily with marketing his wares.

But since printmaking has and will continue to have some connection with business, it behooves the artist to minimize the commercial involvement by adopting a uniform code of practice. In so doing, he will not only lighten his own load of perplexing detail by transforming it into routine procedure; he will also help to raise standards in the art market. An organization composed exclusively of artists, known as the International Association of Plastic Arts, a UNESCO affiliate, adopted a resolution, at its Third International Congress at Vienna in 1960, defining original prints, or *estampes originales*. The text of the resolution and another by the French print organization are reprinted at the end of this section. The Print Council, in consultation with its members, including a number of prominent printmakers, has assembled further commentary and clarification of the resolution. These notes are hereby offered to all printmakers in the hope that they will find the suggestions fair, wise, and practical. Here, then, is a program formulated by artists and their well-wishers, designed to enhance the prestige and integrity of original prints. It is hoped that all printmakers will accept the code, and, what is equally important, adhere to it.

ORIGINAL PRINTS. In original prints, the artist is both the designer and executant; he performs every step in the creation of the master design on a suitable medium from which the prints are pulled. It is not essential that original prints be limited in edition. And here the Print Council differs from the recommendation of the International Association of Plastic Arts, which recognizes as original only those that bear "an indication of the total edition and the serial number of the print." Where the edition is not specified, it is limited only by the number of perfect proofs that can be pulled—a question that can wisely be left to the judgment and integrity of the artist himself. The artist in the creation of his master design is free to use any tools or means at his disposal. In addition to traditional methods, he has used such modern devices as welding, electric drills, plastics, radioactive isotopes. Although direct photography and the exclusive reliance on photomechanical plates are frowned upon by most printmakers, fragments, such as parts of halftone blocks or so-called *newspaper mat*, have been applied as impresses on plates or lithographic stones, and further manipulated by hand. Artists have sometimes combined several mediums in one print. The Print

Council has no desire to tell the artist how to work. The creator alone sets the norm and justifies the means.

PRINTING. Although many artists are scrupulous about executing all the steps in the making of a print, including the printing, it is not imperative that the printing be done by the artist in order to produce an original print. It can be done by a professional or a pupil working under the supervision of the master. What is important is that the printing be of good quality, on good paper, and up to the standard demanded by the artist. If the printing is actually done by the artist, it is suggested that he indicate the fact by adding the letters *imp.* after his pencil signature.

TRIAL PROOFS. While an artist is working on his plate, wood block, or stone, he sometimes inks and pulls an impression to see how his work has progressed. Such prints are called trial proofs, and should be so marked. Because they represent various unfinished states, they should not be considered as part of the finished edition.

ARTIST'S PROOFS. Originally and theoretically, an artist's proof was one outside the regular quota or edition, and reserved for the artist's personal use (for instance, presentation to a friend). A very small number were so designated, and an artist's proof, if and when it came on the market, acquired the added value of personal association. In recent years the practice of marking artist's proofs has been abused. An artist recently published a print in a limited edition of fifteen, numbering each print. Through a misunderstanding, one of his assistants who did the printing printed fifty extra proofs. These were marked artist's proofs and are being sold as such. The printing of practically as many artist's proofs as are included in the published edition is fairly common. In view of the abuse or misunderstanding of the original intention, it would be desirable to establish some standard procedure. It is, of course, quite legitimate for an artist to keep a few proofs, or as many as he wants, for himself. But if he issues a limited and numbered edition without a public record of the number of artist's proofs, there is the possibility of a half-truth causing misinformation. The British Section of the International Association of Plastic Arts recommends that the number of artist's proofs be limited to 10 percent of the total edition. This figure, or perhaps a maximum of five when editions are small, could be set as the norm. Any amount over that number should be considered as part of the regular edition, and added to the total count as the final edition number.

SIGNING PRINTS. The custom of publishing only prints signed in pencil has become well established. The signature has come to stand for, among other things, a guarantee of printing quality, a stamp of good workmanship, similar to the hallmark on silver. It would be improper, therefore, for the artist to sign a reproduction, unless it is clearly marked as such; or to sign inferior prints, which were printed, in quantity, from books or periodicals.

NUMBERING PRINTS. This again has become a well-established custom. There are confusion and superstition regarding the value of numbering in sequence. It is often assumed that the earliest proofs are the best. This is not necessarily true in view of the small editions usually printed today. The assumption would be most likely to be valid with regard to drypoint, since the burr wears down rapidly. It used to be standard practice among professional etchers to steel-face the copper-plate of a drypoint as soon as the design was completed, thereby preventing it from wearing down. There is no reason to believe that this tradition has been completely neglected. Wood blocks would show little wear within the limits of impressions of one hundred or so. It often takes a number of printings for a stone to be worked into its proper form. And, likewise, it may take a number of proofs before the printmaker discovers the right combination of ink, paper, and handling that will bring out the best in an intaglio plate. Other things being equal, "happy accident" plays an important role. Therefore it happens that sometimes the early and sometimes the later proofs are best. Even if the printer is scrupulous in maintaining the proper sequence of a series of black-and-white prints, when there are several printings, as in a color print, the true order is bound to be jumbled. Numbering prints has become an established custom, without real significance except for the purpose of making sales. Perhaps the artists as a group could take some concerted action regarding the problem.

LIMITING EDITIONS. Editions of prints do not have to be limited, and were not limited in the past. The editions are smaller today than they were in the past, perhaps because so many modern artists do their own printing and are reluctant to spend too much of their time printing. But if it is claimed that an edition is limited, it must be limited in fact. Each print should bear an indication of the maximum size of the edition. It follows that the artist may be free to print less, but not more, than the number specified.

CANCELLATION. When the total edition has been printed, it is advisable for the artist to destroy the master design: efface the image in the case of a lithographic stone, or cancel the plate or other material, in order that no unauthorized prints can be taken. Cancellation may be effected by gouging arbitrary lines into the plane surface, drilling holes through it, or by altering the shape of the plate in such a way as to alter the design; for example, on a rectangular plate, a corner containing part of the image may be distinctly altered from a right angle to a curve.

DATING PRINTS. In this suggestion, we hear the curator and the scholar voicing the hope that the artist will date each print at the time he makes it.

DRAFT OF RESOLUTION
adopted by the Third International Congress of Plastic Arts,
Vienna, September 1960

ORIGINAL PRINTS

1. It is the exclusive right of the artist-printmaker to fix the definitive number of each of his graphic works in the different techniques: engraving, lithography, etc.

2. Each print, in order to be considered an original, must bear not only the signature of the artist, but also an indication of the total edition and the serial number of the print.

The artist may also indicate that he himself is the printer.[a]

3. Once the edition has been made, it is desirable that the original plate, stone, woodblock, or whatever material was used in pulling the print edition, should be defaced or should bear a distinctive mark indicating that the edition has been completed.

4. The above principles apply to graphic works which can be considered originals, that is to say to prints for which the artist made the original plate, cut the woodblock, worked on the stone or on any other material. Works which do not fulfill these conditions must be considered "reproductions."

5. For reproductions no regulations are possible. However, it is desirable that reproductions should be acknowledged as such, and so distinguished beyond question from original graphic work. This is particularly so when reproductions are of such outstanding quality that the artist, wishing to acknowledge the work materially executed by the printer, feels justified in signing them.

Note (a): In the United States of America, when the artist himself is the printer he places the letters "Imp." (*impressit*, he printed it) after his signature.

ACTION BY THE NATIONAL COMMITTEE ON ENGRAVING

as reported in *Nouvelles de l'Estampe*, February, 1965

The following definition of Original Engraving was adopted by the National Committee on Engraving at its general meeting on December 18, 1964:

"*La Chambre Syndicale de l'Estampe et du Dessin*, in view of the lack of legislation for the protection of the Original Print, and of the use of this designation, directs the attention of print dealers, as well as of the public forming their clientele, to the fact that the definition of an Original Print—which has served as the basis of the pertinent text drawn up by the French Customs Service, and which was formulated by the National Committee on Engraving at the International Exposition of 1937 under the presidency of M. Marcel Guiot and in turn adopted by the National Committee on Engraving under the presidency of M. Julien Cain—reads as follows:

" 'Proofs either in black or in color, drawn from one or several plates, conceived and executed entirely by hand by the same artist, regardless of the technique employed, with the exclusion of any and all mechanical or photomechanical processes, shall be considered original engravings, prints, or lithographs.'

"Only prints meeting such qualifications are entitled to be designated Original Prints."

VI

The Dealer and the Print Market

THE QUALIFICATIONS OF A DEALER

THE DEALER is the intermediary between the artist and the collector. What are the qualifications of a good dealer? First of all, one might say: experience. And experience implies many things. For instance, an interest in and knowledge of his field, whether it be prints or paintings or whatever. This does not mean that he should take a number of art courses (though a few might help), but that he should be able to look at prints, day in and day out—and like it. The study of prints is in itself a liberal education; and the continuous examination of whatever turns up—good, bad, indifferent, and even spurious—gives him a grasp of the field quite different from that of an art course with slides. Experience generally comes from apprenticeship with an older dealer or an older establishment. With experience comes a sense of obligation and responsibility.

In boom times and a seller's market, almost anyone can set

up as a dealer and make a success of it, with no experience and few qualifications except a glib tongue. But then, at some time or another, he might sell, for a high price, a picture that proves to be a forgery. Not only is he in trouble through his inexperience; he has given the whole profession a black eye. There is a saying, "It pays to be ignorant," and perhaps it is true that one can put across a deal with greater assurance if one has no doubts or reservations. But it does not pay in the long run. The honorable dealer has an obligation to give his client the benefit of his experience; and he would much prefer a long-enduring relationship with his client, on the basis of confidence and trust, than a fly-by-night success. Indeed, the dealer has a wonderful opportunity to educate the taste of his customers, provided he has standards of his own. He should have pride in his own profession, and weigh the advantage of a long-range program against the opportunity to make a quick turnover. It is to his advantage to inoculate his client with the "collector's itch," so that he will come back for more. If, however, he continually takes advantage of the customer's confidence to sell him a dubious bill of goods, sooner or later the day of reckoning will come, and the client will reflect ruefully on that sharp-edged maxim *Caveat emptor*, "Let the buyer beware."

There is another proverb that is sometimes quoted in criticism of business practice, namely, the old maxim of the antiquarian dealer, "Buy cheap, and sell dear." In view of the great publicity given now to the prices of art objects, and the fact that the art market is becoming more and more international, the maxim has lost much of its point. There are no countries or general sources where the dealer could pick up bargains to sell at a high price. The problem of the dealer today is not to sell pictures but to obtain pictures to sell. He cannot hope to get them at less than a fair price.

AUCTIONS

There is another form of commerce in prints, namely, sales at auction. There are auction houses of good repute that make some attempt to catalogue their wares correctly, and there are others that are not averse to shady deals. And there are of course many auction houses, specializing in furniture and furnishings from estates, that may sell prints "as is" or without any listing at all. There are many people whose concern with prints is peripheral and whose ignorance, consequently, is without intent to defraud. In general, auction houses sell without guarantee, and the bidder takes his chances. At an auction sale the dealer of course knows what he wants and what is good. In America, auction houses are much frequented by collectors and amateurs. In this sense, the auction houses are in competition with the dealers for the purchasing power of the public. Furthermore, a customer may come to a dealer for advice about an item at auction, or even ask the dealer to buy it for him at the sale. This puts the dealer in an embarrassing situation, for he might have wanted to buy the print himself, especially if, by chance, it goes for a song. Even if the dealer does buy the print for his customer as a favor, he should charge a commission for his services, usually 10 percent of the outside limit of the bid, no matter what the print actually will bring at the auction. The dealer is giving good service for his fee, since he, in a way, is guaranteeing the quality and authenticity of the print, as well as advising how much should be paid for it.

APPRAISALS

Another service often asked of the dealer is the appraisal of prints for insurance or tax-deductible purposes. Appraisals can be a nuisance from the dealer's point of view. They are time-consuming. The layman, for instance, who has found a picture in the attic and is convinced (often in a long-winded

[93]

way) that it must be worth a mint of money does not realize how much he imposes on the good nature of the dealer. Appraisal also involves liability: The dealer is accountable for his evaluations, even at times to the extent of appearance in court. To meet this problem, the dealers have banded together in the Art Dealers Association of America, Inc. (575 Madison Avenue, New York), to which they refer all requests for appraisal, and which charges a sizable fee for its services. This works very well when the stakes are high, as in a painting or antique furniture, but would not hold for run-of-mill prints where the top valuation might be less than the fee charged.

The print dealers are still saddled with a problem; and each one must decide how much time he can devote to the cultivation of business goodwill in irrelevant matters. The museum print rooms have shouldered a part of the burden by their so-called collectors' clinics, where the public may bring works for identification and authentication. But the curators, by museum regulations, are not allowed to make monetary valuations of works of art. Auction houses are in the habit of making appraisals, but again there is a question as to what extent they can perform the service gratuitously or without commitment to place the object for sale at auction. For the general public—ignorant of prices but prone to exaggeration, suspicious of being defrauded—the situation presents a genuine problem: Where can it turn to get an honest appraisal? There seems to be no conclusive answer. Perhaps the only hope for the collector is to encounter an honorable dealer who will give fair advice or valuation.

A CODE OF STANDARDS

So much for the dealer in general, his ideal qualifications, and some of the services he can or might render. These considerations are largely a background for the question at issue. The Print Council is trying to correct some abuses that have arisen during the last thirty years in the sale of original prints and certain imitations offered as originals. The Council is enlisting the aid of the public through education, and of the artists and dealers through the establishment of a flexible and workable code of standards. With the aid of an advisory committee of dealers, it has formulated the simple code that is printed below. Dealers throughout the country who have subscribed to this code are listed in a special booklet (to be obtained from the Print Council of America, Inc., 527 Madison Avenue, New York, N.Y. 10022). They constitute the body of "qualified" dealers in sympathy with the aims and objectives of the Print Council, and are entitled to display the certificate from the Council testifying to their adherence to the code of standards.

Another weapon in the campaign against misrepresentation is customs inspection of importations. In our tariff law, reproductions of all kinds are dutiable, whereas original prints are duty free. If a customs declaration states that a print is a reproduction, the importer, and anyone cognizant of the same fact, would be committing a fraud if he sold it as an original print. Furthermore, if he enters, in a customs declaration, a print as original, while knowing that it is not, his conduct is fraudulent and actionable. The text of the pertinent provisions of the Tariff Act and Regulations is printed below.

TARIFF ACT AND REGULATIONS

After providing that unbound etchings, engravings, woodcuts, lithographs and prints made by other hand transfer processes may enter free of duty, Par. 1807 of the Tariff Act defines these prints as including "only such as are printed by hand from plates, stones, or blocks etched, drawn, or engraved with hand tools and not such as are printed from plates, stones, or blocks etched, drawn, or engraved by photochemical or other mechanical processes."

The pertinent regulation (Par. 10.48) provides in part as follows:

10.48 Original paintings, engravings, drawings, sculpture, etc.

(*a*) Invoices covering works of art claimed to be free of duty under paragraph 1807, Tariff Act of 1930, as amended, shall show whether they are originals, replicas, reproductions, or copies, and also the name of the artist who produced them, unless upon examination the appraiser is satisfied that such statement is not necessary to a proper determination of the facts.

(*b*) The following evidence shall be filed in connection with the entry:

(1) A declaration in the following form by the artist who produced the article, showing whether it is original; . . . and in the case of etchings, engravings, woodcuts, lithographs, or prints made by other hand transfer processes, that they were printed by hand from hand-etched, hand-drawn, or hand-engraved plates, stones, or blocks:

I, ..., do hereby declare that I am the painter or producer of certain works of art, viz.: . . . . covered by the annexed invoice dated . . . .; . . . . and that the said etchings, engravings, woodcuts, lithographs, or prints made by other hand transfer processes were printed by hand from hand-etched, hand-drawn, or hand-engraved plates, stones, or blocks.

(2) A declaration of the seller or shipper giving the information specified in (1), if it be shown that it is impossible to produce the declaration of the artist.

(3) A declaration of the importer on customs Form 3307.

(*c*) The declaration of the artist, or the declaration of the seller or shipper in lieu thereof, may be waived upon a satisfactory showing that it is impossible to produce either, but the declaration of the importer shall be required in all cases.

(*d*) Artists' proof etchings, engravings, woodcuts, lithographs, or prints made by other hand transfer processes should bear the genuine signature or mark of the artist as evidence of their authenticity, in the absence of such a signature or mark, other evidence shall be required which will establish the authenticity of the work to the satisfaction of the collector.

CODE OF DEALERS' STANDARDS

1. A dealer should not describe any print as an original print, original etching, original lithograph, original engraving, original woodcut or the like, unless it is an original print as defined below.

2. A dealer should deliver to a buyer a written invoice for prints sold, distinguishing reproductions from original prints in all printed matter, including catalogs, advertisements, and upon all invoices.

3. Catalog descriptions of prints should include all pertinent and significant information available with respect to such matters as collaboration on plate, signature or numbering by others than the artist, processes used and who used them, condition of print (such as cut margin or restoration), states, size of edition and number of impression, signature, date of execution, date of impression, cancellation of plate. Such information shall be conveyed to the buyer and shall, upon request, be entered on the invoice.

4. Dealers should use their best efforts to obtain from artists, publishers, and other sources, and to make available to the public, evidence that work is original; a description of how each print was made; and other pertinent facts such as catalog information and number.

5. Dealers should help members of the public to understand the difference between a reproduction and an original print, explaining processes of printmaking and using their best efforts to foster knowledge and appreciation of fine prints, new and old, avoiding unusual and misleading terms such as "heliograph" which

conceal the fact that a reproduction is not an original print.

An **original print** is a work of art, the general requirements of which are:

1. The artist alone has created the master image in or upon the plate, stone, wood block or other material, for the purpose of creating the print.

2. The print is made from the said material, by the artist or pursuant to his directions.

3. The finished print is approved by the artist.

These requirements define the original print of today and do not in all cases apply to prints made before 1930.

VII

The Care and Conservation
of Fine Prints

by CHRISTA M. GAEHDE

MANY FINE PRINTS have survived in pristine condition for centuries, but many more have been damaged and lost through neglect and ill treatment. The curator or conservator through whose hands pass prints of all periods is unhappily aware that even today irreplaceable prints—old and modern alike—are ruined by improper handling, faulty mounting, matting, and framing, by overexposure to light and unfavorable climatic conditions, and by well-intentioned but ill-advised and unskilled "restoration."

It is the purpose of the following pages to alert the interested public to the principal causes of destruction and disintegration, and to recommend practical measures to avoid unnecessary loss.[1]

---

[1] For a bibliography and a discussion of the present state of knowledge in the field of paper conservation, see L. Santucci, "The Application of Chemical and Physical Methods to Conservation of Archival Materials," *Recent Advances in Conservation* (Contributions to the IIC Rome Conference, 1961, ed. G. Thomson) (London, 1963), pp. 39–47.

HANDLING OF PRINTS. Loose prints should be handled as little as possible and only with clean hands. When it is necessary to lift unmounted prints, they should be held with two hands. Prints on particularly thin and fragile paper should be carried laid flat on clean cardboard.

TEARS. If a print is accidentally torn, the tear should not be touched. Handling will dirty the edges and thus make repairs more difficult. The torn print should be laid between two smooth and clean cardboards and protected from dust until it can be repaired by an expert paper restorer. Any "first aid" by the amateur will increase the damage.

PROTECTION OF PRINT SURFACE. In order to avoid rubbing of delicate surfaces, loose prints should never be stacked on top of each other or kept in portfolios unless they are separated by guard sheets of tissue or, preferably, glassine paper.[2] No paper of inferior quality should be used. Low-grade paper containing ground wood and acid fillers deteriorates rapidly and will stain and embrittle the paper of the print with which it is in contact.

MATS. The best safeguard against physical damage is the traditional mat, provided it is correctly made and safe materials are used. The collector or owner who will have to rely on commercial framers to have his prints matted is cautioned to insist on the following points:

QUALITY OF MAT BOARD. Only 100 percent rag-fiber mat stock is to be used.[3] All-rag board has a good resistance to

[2] Suppliers of glassine paper: Fort Hill Paper Co., 309 Beacon Street, Somerville 45, Mass.; Bulkley-Dunton Linde Lathrop, Inc., 295 Madison Avenue, New York, N.Y. 10017.

[3] Suppliers of 100 percent rag-fiber mat stock: Andrews-Nelson-Whitehead Paper Co., 7 Laight Street, New York, N.Y.; T. Bainbridge's Sons, 20 Cumberland Street, Brooklyn, N.Y.; Colonial Paper Co., 201/207 Purchase Street, Boston, Mass.; Zellerbach Paper Company, 245 South Spruce Avenue, South San Francisco, Calif.

aging and, if kept in proper climatic conditions, is reasonably safe from microbiological attack by cellulose-degenerating bacteria and fungi causing what is commonly known as "foxing" and "mildew." Less resistant low-grade boards—all too often used by framers—may act as host to parasitic organisms that will attack the print. Furthermore, inferior board will stain and corrode the print at the same rate as the board itself deteriorates.

OLD MATS. An old mat acquired with a print may be of historical interest or aesthetic value. It may contain notations or marks of famous collectors or it may be a decorative mat of the eighteenth or nineteenth century. If such mats have not appreciatively aged or discolored and show no signs of microbiological infection, they were obviously made of stable materials and can be reused after cleaning of surface dust. However, to ensure maximum safety it may be advisable to replace the old backboard, or rear board, with a new all-rag board and to insert a 1-ply rag frame between the old frame and the print.

NEW DECORATIVE MATS. If new decorative or "French" mats are desired, they should be made of all-rag board. The board, usually off-white in color, can be either colored directly or lined with a colored rag paper of good quality.

CONSTRUCTION OF MAT. A mat consists of a supporting board and a covering frame of varying width, whose window, or aperture, displays the print. Support and frame are connected or hinged on the long side either at the left or at the top, according to the format of the print. This arrangement allows the opening of the mat to expose the whole of the print to examination (Figure 1). The best material for connecting

Figure 1   Mat opened

Frame board

Linen tape hinge

Backboard

Frame Board

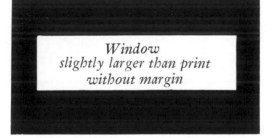

Window
slightly larger than print
without margin

Linen tape hinge

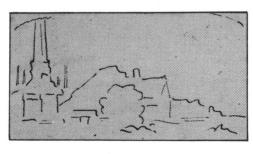

Backboard

backboard and frame is gummed white linen tape.[4] Brown or gray paper tape or any kind of "sticky" tape are to be avoided.

SIZE OF MAT. The size and format of the mat depend on the size and format of the print, and should strike a proper balance between aesthetic considerations and protective function. Collectors may find it practical to standardize the sizes of their mats for easier storage. The sizes most commonly used by museums are: 30 by 40, 22 by 28, 16 by 22, and 14¼ by 19¼ or 14 by 18 inches.

PLACING AND SIZE OF WINDOW. It is general practice to place the window, or aperture, in the optical center of the mat instead of the mathematical center. The lower frame of the cover mat is thus slightly higher than the upper frame, which is more satisfying to the eye than having all four sides of the frame of equal width.

The size of the window is naturally adjusted to the size of the printed image. It is desirable, however, to allow for a blank interval of aesthetically appropriate width between the inner edge of the cover frame and the outer edge of the image. Prints that have no margin are thus made to "float" in the window, and are not covered or touched by the cover frame of the mat.

In the case of prints with margin, some width of the margin is allowed to show all around, especially that which may contain the artist's signature, title, or other information.

The mat maker's knife leaves sharp edges. To prevent prints from being cut by the edges of the window, these edges should be slightly blunted with fine sandpaper or a very fine file.

[4] Suppliers of gummed linen tape: Gane Brothers and Co., Inc., 480 Canal Street, New York, N.Y. 10013; Gaylord Bros., 155 Gifford Street, Syracuse, N.Y.

THICKNESS OF MAT. The protective purpose of the mat is served only if the mat board's thickness is in proper relation to the size and fragility of the print. All-rag matting board is produced in 1-ply, 2-ply, or 4-ply thicknesses. Obviously, a large print requires the stiff support of 4-ply sheets for backboard and frame. For smaller sizes a 2-ply thickness may be sufficient, except in instances where the print surface is in heavy relief; 4-ply mats are preferable in general, but lower cost and economy of storage space may favor 2-ply mats. Board of 1 ply is not recommended.

METHODS OF HINGING THE PRINT. The function of the hinge is to affix the print to the backboard of the mat. There are various methods of hinging. The print may either be hinged at the left side or at the top, depending on its format and corresponding to the hinge of the mat (Figure 2). If the matted print belongs to a study collection and is stored horizontally, hinging at the side is preferable because it makes for easier and safer handling. If the print is to be framed or to be exhibited in a vertical position, it should have its hinges at the top regardless of format. For small prints two hinges are sufficient. Larger prints require three or more hinges. Very large or heavy prints that may easily slip from the usual fold hinges should be provided with pendant-type hinges (Figure 3).

Prints without margin that are made to "float" in the window of the mat and that are meant to be framed or exhibited vertically should have hinges at both sides and at top and bottom near the corners. Such prints may also be hinged all around the entire length and width of their edges.

Where prints are not expected to remain in the same mat for a long time, it is advisable to hinge them to sheets of rag paper and to hinge the paper to the mat. This will avoid the necessity of putting new hinges on the print when the mat is changed.

Figure 2   Hinging of print

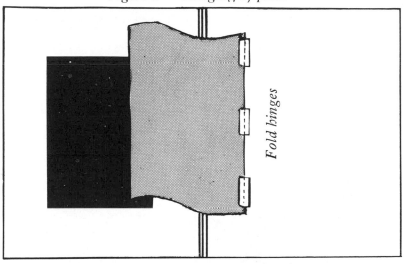

Fold hinges

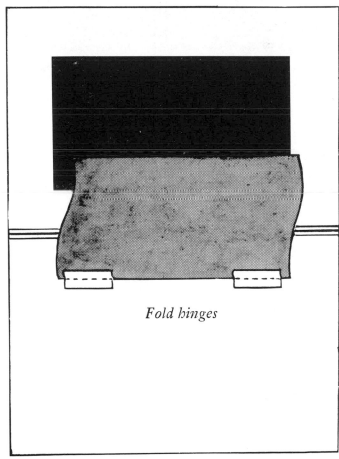

Fold hinges

Figure 3

*Pendant hinges for large or
heavy prints*

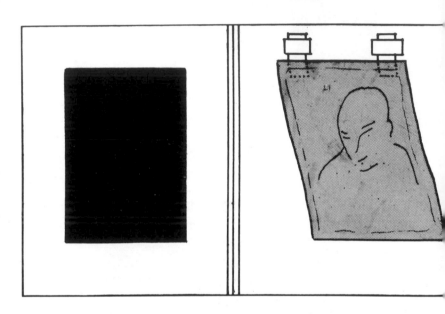

PAPER FOR HINGING. It is imperative that safe materials be used for hinging. The best is tough-fibered Japanese paper that should not exceed the thickness or strength of the paper of the print so that, when under strain, it will give way before the print itself tears. Commercially available paper tapes, such as Dennison Transparent Mending Tape or the hinges used by stamp collectors, are feasible but not recommended because they tend to come loose when they dry out. Framers should especially be warned against the convenient but deplorable use of gummed paper tapes or adhesive plastic tapes such as Scotch Tape or masking tape. These materials are very harmful. Paper tape deteriorates and stains the print, and the adhesive substance of the plastic tapes penetrates into the paper and hardens, leaving ugly stains that are very difficult to remove.

ADHESIVE FOR HINGING. For the same reason, no glues or synthetic adhesives, such as rubber cement, should be used to affix the hinges. Though regular white library paste is better, it is not recommended. To have a paste that is absolutely free from staining material and harmful preservatives, it is best to prepare it yourself.

The most simple among various recipes [5] is made up of 1 ounce (4 heaped teaspoons) of rice starch to 1 pint of cold water. The starch is mixed with a little of the cold water to a thick cream in a clean aluminum or enamel pan. The rest of the water is brought to a boil in another pan and—under continued stirring—added to the mixture over moderate heat until the paste thickens and takes on a glassy appearance. This paste is safe to use for about two days if kept covered in normal temperature of about 65° F. It should be thrown away as soon as it becomes sour and watery. The addition of one teaspoon of liquid Formalin stirred in as a preservative after the mixture is removed from the fire will prolong usefulness up to three or four days.

APPLICATION OF ADHESIVE TO HINGE. The paste should be applied evenly and thinly to the hinges so that it will not penetrate through the Japanese paper and cause the folded hinges to stick together. It is also advisable to leave the outer edges of the hinge free from paste. This allows easy removal, if necessary, by pulling up on the free edge and toward the fold.

[5] See G. L. Stout and M. H. Horwitz, "Experiments with Adhesives for Paper," *Technical Studies in the Field of the Fine Arts*, III, 1 (July, 1934), 38–64.

PROTECTIVE SHEET FOR MATTED PRINT. To protect the surface of the matted print against scratches and abrasion as well as against dust while in storage, a glassine paper slightly less than the size of the whole mat should be laid between the print and the mat frame. Although this paper is not fully transparent, it is, according to present experience, safer than most translucent materials. (For translucent cover sheets, see STORAGE OF PRINTS.)

FINAL CAUTION TO PICTURE FRAMER AND MAT MAKER. Finally, the picture framer or mat maker should be emphatically warned never to cut the print's margins to fit a frame or mat. He is to leave the print in exactly the condition in which he received it for matting. He should not tear or soak off old hinges. He should not attempt any repairs or cleaning to cover up accidental damage. He should not try to flatten the print by "pressing" or "ironing." Under no circumstances should he mount—that is, paste or dry-mount—the print to the supporting mat board or any other kind of board or paper. (See also WARPING OF FRAMED PRINTS.) All such work, if necessary, should be entrusted only to an expert paper restorer.

HANDLING OF MATTED PRINTS. Students handling matted prints should be cautioned to lift the mat with both hands. Lifting with one hand strains mat and print and may cause the hinges to tear. When you open the mat, turn the cover frame over by holding its outside edge and not the edge of the window. The frequent bad practice of opening the mat by putting a finger through the window endangers the print.

STORAGE OF MATTED PRINTS. The safest, most convenient receptacles for the horizontal storage of matted prints are

Solander boxes lined with all-rag paper on the inside.[6] The Solander box consists of a case with a hinged back that falls to a horizontal position when the box is opened. This device allows you to take the matted prints out by sliding them from box to lid and back. Naturally, the internal measurements of the Solander box should be slightly larger than the size of the mat. The box may hold from seventeen to twenty matted prints, depending on the thickness of the mats.

Large mats, 30 by 40 or 22 by 28 inches in size, may be kept in portfolios or simply shelved in closed drawers.

CONSERVATION OF OVERSIZE POSTERS. Oversize prints, such as nineteenth- and twentieth-century posters, present a special conservation and storage problem. They are easily damaged because of their size; and their paper, frequently of inferior quality, may have become embrittled with age even under favorable climatic conditions. If possible, such prints should be deacidified and reinforced with a strong backing by an experienced worker. Muslin and linen are often used for this purpose, and have given satisfactory results where the paper is still sufficiently strong and thick. However, the textiles themselves are subject to aging and deterioration, and have a different ratio of expansion and contraction than paper when exposed to atmospheric changes. This frequently results in tensions between paper and backing that may produce rippling and subsequent breaking of the paper. Furthermore, the pressure applied during the mounting process may impress the texture of the textile through the surface of the print. Tough-fibered Japanese paper is a much better medium for backing.

[6] Suppliers of Solander boxes: Cambridge Paper Box Co., Cambridge 39, Mass.; Spink & Gaborc, Inc., 26 East Thirteenth Street, New York, N.Y. 10003; The Mosette Co., 28 East Twenty-second Street, New York, N.Y. 10010.

It has a generally good resistance to aging, and the great many varieties available permit the selection of a paper that has a ratio of expansion and contraction corresponding to that of the poster. The adhesive to be used for the joining of poster and backing is the paste of rice starch recommended for hinging. (See ADHESIVE FOR HINGING.)

The mounted posters should be shelved horizontally. Truly man-sized posters are suspended from hangers.

STORAGE OF PRINTS WITHOUT MAT; TRANSPARENT SHEETS. The Tamarind Lithography Workshop, Inc., recently drew attention to the fact that many contemporary artists produce large prints without margin, or consider the margin as part of the print's aesthetic effect. The matting of such prints is considered to be contrary to the artists' intentions. Therefore, the Tamarind Workshop advises the laying of such prints on a backing of board of the same size as the print, and then enclosing the print and its backing in plastic or cellophane. This procedure is admissible only if safe transparent sheets are used.

Celluloid (nitrocellulose) is highly dangerous because it is inflammable; it also darkens on exposure to light, and frees nitric acid, which destroys paper. Cellophane and cellulose acetate are moderately stable, but cellulose acetate butyrate (CAB)[7] is more durable. Among the polyethylene (polythene) plastics, only polyethylene terephthalate sheets (related to Dacron) are reasonably safe, although they are sensitive to ultraviolet light and should not be exposed to direct sunlight.[8]

[7] Cellulose acetate butyrate (CAB) sheets are produced by Eastman Chemical Products, Inc., Kingsport, Tenn., under the trade name Kodacel B2X.

[8] Polyethylene terephthalate sheets are produced by E. I. du Pont de Nemours, Inc., Wilmington, Del., under the trade name Mylar, and by Imperial Chemical Industries, Ltd., 488 Madison Avenue, New York, N.Y., under the trade name Melinex.

(See EXPOSURE TO LIGHT.) The most durable are the acrylic sheets, particularly Plexiglas (polymethyl methacrylate), which is produced in thicknesses from 1.5 to 25.0 mm. These sheets, however, have the disadvantage of being easily scratched, and they attract dust because of static electricity. This latter condition, however, can be remedied by applying an antistatic coating supplied by the manufacturer.[9]

These materials should not be made into airtight envelopes for prints because they may trap condensed moisture, which is very harmful. (See AIR CONDITIONING.) It is sufficient to hinge the print to an adequately stiff all-rag board of identical or slightly larger size, and to cover it with a sheet of plastic affixed to the upper edge of the support. For the purpose of storage, glassine paper, instead of plastic, provides the same protection at less cost.

STORAGE CONDITIONS. Protection against polluted air, as well as control of temperature and humidity, is absolutely necessary for the preservation of works of art on paper.[10]

POLLUTION. The air of cities and industrial areas contains harmful concentrations of sulfur dioxide gas produced by the combustion of coal and other fuels. These fumes are absorbed by the paper, where they combine with the oxygen and moisture of the air to accumulate sulfuric acid, which decomposes the fibrous structure of the paper.

EMBRITTLEMENT BY HEAT AND DRYNESS. Temperature and humidity have an immediate effect on paper, and are important factors in the control of microbiological infection. Exposure to high temperatures above 75° F. and to relative humidity

[9] Plexiglas sheets are produced by Rohm & Haas Company, Washington Square, Philadelphia 5, Pa.

[10] See H. J. Plenderleith and P. Philippot, "Climatology and Conservation in Museums," *Museum* (UNESCO), XIII, 1960, 201–289.

below 30 percent dries and embrittles paper and will hasten the process of aging, whereas lower temperatures have a retarding effect when relative humidity is kept at about 50 percent. Most papers are at their greatest mechanical strength when their moisture content is in equilibrium with air of 50 to 65 percent relative humidity.

CHANGES IN TEMPERATURE AND HUMIDITY. The atmospheric fluctuations all too familiar in America's climate cause paper fibers to expand with moisture and to contract with dryness. Prints may not remain flat under such conditions, but are apt to warp, buckle, or throw "waves." If this occurs too frequently, internal and external friction may ultimately have some detrimental effect on the print. (See WARPING OF FRAMED PRINTS.)

MICROBIOLOGICAL INFECTION. Moisture also favors the growth of harmful microbiological organisms that will thrive if the print is exposed to relative humidities above 75 percent even for a short period. At a relative humidity of 50 to 65 percent and temperatures up to 65° F., fungi are not expected to become active, although the spores are present in the air and particularly in dust.

DUST. Dust is not only one of the major carriers of microorganisms; it also has a detrimental mechanical effect on paper. Its sharp-edged particles penetrate into the paper and have a cutting and scouring effect. Once these particles are firmly embedded, they cannot be removed by soft erasers or by washing. Dust should never be allowed to accumulate, and periodical vacuum cleaning of shelves is strongly recommended.

AIR CONDITIONING. Constant air conditioning is the best

protection against the dangers described above. Dehumidifiers may be sufficient where temperature can be controlled by other means. Where such equipment is not in use, careful ventilation may reduce some of the hazards. Air may be circulated by strategically placed fans. Windows should be opened on dry days only. In small closed areas a dehydrating agent, such as anhydrous calcium chloride, silica gel, kaken gel, or other "humidity-storing" salts, placed in flat open pans may help to control moisture.

CURATIVE AND PREVENTIVE TREATMENT OF MICROBIOLOGICAL INFECTION. The curative treatment of fungus-infected prints demands expert advice and help because of the need for proper fumigation equipment, specialized knowledge, and the high toxicity of the effective fungicides.[11] Preventive measures, however, can be taken by placing open containers of paradichlorobenzene crystals upon the storage shelves. This chemical has a mild fungicidal and insecticidal effect.

PEST CONTROL. Experts should also be called upon for the extermination of invasions of paper-destroying insects (silverfish, termites, woodworms, cockroaches, book lice). Commercial exterminators should be warned to use insecticides that will neither stain paper nor have any other adverse effect on the stored prints.[12]

EXPOSURE TO LIGHT. Prints framed under glass and exhibited in the home or in a gallery are exposed to the additional danger of the deteriorating effect of light. The radiant energy of visible light—not only of ultraviolet rays—causes a decomposition of the molecular structure of paper that manifests

[11] See F. Gallo, "Biological Agents Which Damage Paper Materials in Libraries and Archives," *Recent Advances in Conservation*, pp. 55–61.
[12] See P. Gallo, "Problems in the Use of Insecticides on Occupied Premises," *Recent Advances in Conservation*, pp. 48–54.

itself in progressive embrittlement. Depending upon the paper's composition and the circumstances of temperature and humidity, the degenerating process may be accompanied either by the familiar yellowing or by bleaching. Similarly, some pigments, dyes, or inks used in colored prints may react to continued light exposure either by fading or by darkening.

Direct sunlight may cause quite rapid deterioration, especially when the print's paper is of low quality. Nineteenth-century lithographs and posters, for instance, are known to have been severely affected after only a few weeks of exposure. Diffused daylight takes considerably longer to produce the same effect, while fluorescent and—even more—incandescent artificial light drastically diminish the hazard of spectral energy without, however, eliminating it completely.

As a general precaution prints should never be exhibited where direct sunlight can fall on them, and exposure time should be limited by alternating exhibition and dark storage every few months. Collections and galleries that show prints permanently will want to consult scientific reports on museum lighting and the use of filters.[13]

FRAMING OF PRINTS. When having prints framed, particular care should be taken to keep the print well away from the glass because changes of temperature may cause condensation of moisture on the inside of the glass. Water stains and increased vulnerability to microbiological and photochemical harm can be the result of allowing the print to touch the glass. Furthermore, prints may remain firmly stuck to the glass even after the moisture has dried. This can cause severe damage to the surface of the print.

The simplest way to avoid this danger is to protect the print with a sufficiently deep all-rag mat. In the case of prints which are not matted for aesthetical or historical reasons (some mod-

[13] See R. L. Feller, "Control of deteriorating effects of light upon museum objects," *Museum*, XVII, 2, 1964, 57–98. This valuable article also contains all earlier bibliography of importance.

ern and early-American material) a rag-board strip or fillet ought to be inserted between glass and print all around the frame (Figure 4).

Figure 4

Framing of prints without mat

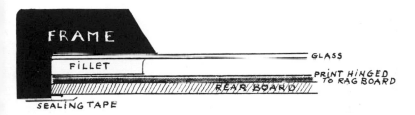

The framing of prints pressed between two sheets of glass is definitely harmful.

PLEXIGLAS. Plexiglas is sometimes used for framing because it is unbreakable. The Plexiglas should be coated with an anti-static to eliminate its tendency to attract dust.[14]

CLOSING AND SEALING OF FRAMES. At this point it bears repetition that the print to be framed must be hinged to all-rag board. (See QUALITY OF MAT BOARD; METHODS OF HINGING THE PRINT.) The board that closes the rear of the frame should preferably also consist of all-rag stock, although a rag-surface pulp-fill board of good quality is generally adequate. The thin wooden boards often found on early-American frames are very harmful because the acid and resinous contents of the

[14] It is inadvisable to use Plexiglas for the framing of pastel, char-coal, and chalk drawings.

[115]

wood will penetrate to the print and in time will stain and deteriorate it.

To eliminate penetration of dust, the frame should be sealed at the back. Gummed linen tape of sufficient width is adequate for this purpose.

VENTILATION OF FRAMED PRINTS. When prints are hung in rooms that are not air-conditioned, it is advisable to fix pieces of cork on the back of the frame at the four corners to allow air to circulate behind the frame.

WARPING OF FRAMED PRINTS. One of the most frequent complaints is that framed prints will not remain flat but will warp, buckle, or throw "waves." This phenomenon, which is due to changes in temperature and relative humidity (see CHANGES IN TEMPERATURE . . .), is certainly undesirable and disturbing. But the "cures" that are too often taken are worse than the complaint. In order to ensure flatness, prints have been brutalized by pasting them on cardboard; they have been dry-mounted to boards by a process that involves the application of heat and pressure; their edges have been pasted or glued all around to a board; and they have been "stretched" over boards or wooden frames as tightly as drumheads.

Each of these measures is harmful to a print. Paper is an organic substance that has its own beauty and life, and its specific qualities are integral to the print's aesthetic effect. The pasting and dry-mounting of prints deprive the paper of its own tensions and its surface freshness. Such "embalmed" prints have lost an essential quality, a fact that is frequently reflected in their reduced market value. The "stretching" of prints is even more deplorable because the paper is still subject to expansion and contraction owing to atmospheric change; but, being imprisoned on all four sides, it cannot obey its own physical impulses. This will cause tensions that weaken its fibrous structure, and may ultimately cause breaking and splitting.

There is only one sure way to avoid the warping of framed prints, and that is to keep the print in the same atmospheric conditions in which it was originally hinged, matted, and framed. Both framers and owners should take cognizance of this fact, although it must be admitted that the rapid fluctuations of the American climate present almost insurmountable difficulties to the observance of this rule. Short of complete air conditioning, the next best thing is to leave the print alone as long as it does not buckle to the extent of rubbing against the glass. It will straighten out with a change of climate; and while such movement is not desirable, it is less harmful than the "cures" described above.

RESTORATION. Proper conservation will greatly diminish the need for restoration. However, if restoration should become necessary, it is wise to consult a paper restorer of acknowledged professional competence and responsibility. After examination of the injured print, the restorer will report on its condition and, if pertinent, on the causes of deterioration. He will outline the methods and the chances of rehabilitation, and submit an estimate of the cost of restoration. The principle that must guide both owner and restorer is to limit restoration to what is absolutely necessary. The safety of the work of art is a more valid consideration than a desire for "rejuvenation" that may turn a mellowed but essentially sound print into an invalid of deceptively "clean" appearance.

PRINT COUNCIL OF AMERICA
527 Madison Avenue
New York City, 10022

A non-profit organization fostering the creation, dissemination, and appreciation of fine prints, new and old.

[119]

William S. Lieberman, New York City
Miss Grace M. Mayer, New York City
A. Hyatt Mayor, New York City
John McKendry, New York City
Kneeland McNulty, Philadelphia, Penn.
Miss Elizabeth Mongan, Pigeon Cove, Mass.
Mrs. Grace McCann Morley, New Delhi, India
Miss Bertha von Moschzisker, Philadelphia, Penn.
Miss Alice Lee Parker, Washington, D.C.
Miss Leona E. Prasse, Cleveland, Ohio
John Rewald, Chicago, Ill.
Jakob Rosenberg, Williamstown, Mass.
Lessing J. Rosenwald, Jenkintown, Penn.
Henry Rossiter, Boston, Mass.
Heinrich Schwarz, Middletown, Conn.
James Thrall Soby, New Canaan, Conn.
E. Gunter Troche, San Francisco, Calif.
Hudson D. Walker, New York City
Robert M. Walker, Swarthmore, Penn.
Peter A. Wick, Cambridge, Mass.
Carl Zigrosser, Philadelphia, Penn.

DECEASED

Arthur A. Heintzelman
Paul J. Sachs
Carl O. Schniewind
Louis E. Stern